FLAVORS OF THE WORLD: A CULINARY JOURNEY THROUGH COUNTRIES

By

Okongor Ndifon

Note: The information in this book is based on the author's research and personal experiences up to the publication date.

Recipes, ingredients, and cooking techniques may evolve over time.

It is always recommended to exercise caution and follow proper food safety guidelines when preparing and consuming dishes.

Dedication:

This book is dedicated to all the passionate food lovers, adventurous cooks, and curious people, who have embarked on a culinary journey through countries of the world.

May you find joy and inspiration in exploring the flavors of the world, embracing diverse cuisines, and creating memorable dining experiences.

To my family and friends, thank you for your unwavering support and for being my taste testers throughout this incredible journey.

Your love and encouragement have fueled my passion for cooking and writing.

To the chefs, home cooks, and culinary artisans around the globe, thank you for sharing your knowledge, traditions, and flavors with the world.

Your dedication to preserving and innovating cuisines has enriched our collective culinary heritage.

And lastly, to the readers of this book, I hope that it sparks your curiosity, broadens your culinary horizons, and encourages you to embark on your own culinary adventures.

May your kitchen be filled with laughter, delicious aromas, and the joy of discovering new flavors.

With heartfelt gratitude,

Okongor Ndifon

Disclaimer:

The recipes and information provided in this book, "Flavors of the World: A Culinary Journey through countries," are intended for informational purposes only.

While every effort has been made to ensure the accuracy of the recipes, ingredient lists, and instructions, the author and publisher cannot guarantee the outcome of the recipes or the suitability of the ingredients for individual dietary needs or restrictions.

Readers are advised to exercise caution and consult a qualified healthcare professional or nutritionist regarding specific dietary concerns, allergies, or food sensitivities.

The author and publisher disclaim any liability for any adverse effects or consequences resulting from the use, preparation, or consumption of the recipes or information provided in this book.

Furthermore, it is the responsibility of the readers to ensure food safety practices, including proper handling, cooking temperatures, and storage of ingredients.

The author and publisher are not liable for any illness, injury, or damage that may occur as a result of improper handling or preparation of ingredients or failure to follow recommended food safety guidelines.

Please note that some recipes may require specialized equipment, techniques, or ingredients that may not be readily available in all regions.

Substitutions and adaptations may be necessary based on personal preferences or ingredient availability.

The author and publisher of this book are not responsible for any changes in recipes, ingredients, or cooking techniques that may occur over time or as a result of individual interpretations or modifications.

By using this book and attempting the recipes within, readers acknowledge and accept the terms of this disclaimer.

TABLE OF CONTENTS

5. African Flavors

- Moroccan Tagines and Couscous
- Ethiopian Injera and Doro Wat
- South African Braai and Bobotie
- Nigerian Jollof Rice and Suya

6. Latin American Delights

- Mexican Tacos and Guacamole
- Argentinian Asado and Empanadas
- Brazilian Feijoada and Brigadeiros
- Peruvian Ceviche and Lomo Saltado

7. Middle Eastern Cuisine

- Lebanese Mezze and Shawarma
- Turkish Kebabs and Baklava
- Israeli Falafel and Hummus
- Iranian Kabobs and Tahdig

8. Oceanic Tastes

- Australian BBQ and Pavlova
- New Zealand Hangi and Kiwi Pies
- Hawaiian Poke and Huli Huli Chicken
- Polynesian Luau and Samoan Palusami

9. Fusion Fare

- Blending Flavors from Around the World

- Creative Recipes and Innovations

10. Sweet Endings

- Decadent Desserts from Different Cultures
- Cakes, Pastries, and Treats

11. Conclusion

- Embrace the Global Gastronomy
- Tips for Hosting International Dinners

12. Appendix

- Conversion Charts
- Glossary of Culinary Terms

13. Recipe Index

1. Introduction

1.11 Welcome to the Culinary Journey Through Countries

Welcome, food enthusiasts, to "Flavors of the World: A Culinary Journey Through Countries"!

Embark on a delightful adventure through the diverse and vibrant cuisines from around the globe.

In this book, we will take you on a gastronomic exploration, uncovering the rich tapestry of flavors, ingredients, and cooking techniques that make each cuisine unique.

Food has an extraordinary power to bring people together, transcending borders and cultures.

It allows us to appreciate the beauty and diversity of the world we live in.

Through this culinary journey, we aim to celebrate the global tapestry of flavors, showcasing the authentic dishes that have been passed down through generations and the innovative creations that blend traditions with modern influences.

Whether you're a seasoned cook looking to expand your repertoire or a curious beginner eager to try new flavors, this book is designed to inspire and empower you in the kitchen.

Each recipe is thoughtfully curated and presented in a way that simplifies the cooking process while ensuring an authentic and satisfying culinary experience.

1.12 About the Author

As the author of "Flavors of the World: A Culinary Journey Through Countries," I am delighted to share my passion for food and culture with you.

My name is Okongor Ndifon, and I have spent time exploring the world through its cuisines.

Through my time, culinary experiences, and deep appreciation for diverse cultures, I have gathered a wealth of knowledge and a collection of recipes that capture the essence of each region.

My journey began as a curious home cook, experimenting with flavors and techniques from different cuisines.

Over time, my love for food evolved into a deeper appreciation for the stories and traditions behind each dish.

I have had the privilege of learning from local cooks, chefs, and home cooks, immersing myself in their culinary heritage, and understanding the significance of food in their lives.

Through this book, I aim to share not only delicious recipes but also the cultural context and personal anecdotes that make each dish special.

My hope is that as you embark on this culinary journey, you will not only discover new recipes but also gain a deeper understanding and appreciation for the people, places, and traditions that inspire them.

So, fasten your aprons and get ready to explore the tantalizing aromas, vibrant colors, and irresistible flavors that await you in "Flavors of the World: A Culinary Journey Through Countries."

Let's embark on this delicious adventure together and savor the richness of global gastronomy.

Happy cooking!

Okongor Ndifon

2. Getting Started

2.11 Essential Ingredients and Tools

Before we dive into the exciting world of global cuisine, let's take a moment to familiarize ourselves with some essential ingredients and tools that will enhance your culinary journey.

These key elements will not only enable you to create authentic flavors but also make your cooking experience more enjoyable and efficient.

I. Essential Ingredients:

a. Herbs and Spices:
Herbs and spices are the backbone of flavor in many cuisines.

Stock your pantry with a variety of aromatic herbs like basil, cilantro, parsley, and mint.

Explore the world of spices, including cumin, coriander, paprika, turmeric, and cinnamon, to name a few.

Each cuisine has its signature spice blends, so don't hesitate to experiment and discover new flavors.

b. Oils and Vinegars:
Olive oil, sesame oil, coconut oil, and vegetable oils are commonly used in different cuisines.

Additionally, vinegars such as balsamic, rice wine vinegar, apple cider vinegar, and lime juice can add acidity and brightness to your dishes.

c. Condiments and Sauces: Condiments like soy sauce, fish sauce,

Worcestershire sauce, and hot sauce can add depth and complexity to your recipes.

Mustard, mayonnaise, and various chutneys and relishes can also provide a burst of flavor.

d. Grains and Legumes:
Rice, pasta, quinoa, lentils, and beans are staple ingredients in many cuisines.

They serve as the foundation for hearty dishes and are versatile enough to be used in a variety of recipes.

e. Proteins:
Depending on dietary preferences, stock up on poultry, beef, pork, fish, tofu, or plant-based proteins like tempeh and seitan.

Each cuisine has its preferred protein sources, so consider exploring local options.

f. Fresh Produce: Fruits and vegetables are essential components of any culinary journey.

From leafy greens and root vegetables to tropical fruits and exotic varieties, fresh produce adds vibrancy and nutrition to your dishes.

II. Tools for Exploring Global Cuisine:

a. Chef's Knife:
A good-quality chef's knife is the workhorse of the kitchen. Invest in a sharp, sturdy knife that feels comfortable in your hand for precise chopping, dicing, and slicing.

b. Cutting Board:

Opt for a durable and spacious cutting board to provide a stable surface for your food preparation.

Consider having separate boards for meats and vegetables to prevent cross-contamination.

c. Cookware:

A versatile set of pots and pans, including a skillet, saucepan, stockpot, and baking sheets, will equip you to prepare a wide range of recipes.

Non-stick pans, cast iron skillets, and stainless steel pots are all valuable additions to your kitchen arsenal.

d. Utensils and Gadgets:

Basic kitchen utensils such as wooden spoons, spatulas, tongs, and a whisk will aid you in various cooking techniques.

Additionally, a thermometer, measuring cups and spoons, a colander, and a can opener are indispensable tools.

e. Blender or Food Processor:

A blender or food processor can simplify tasks like making sauces, purees, and marinades. It is especially useful when working with ingredients that require a smooth texture.

f. Mortar and Pestle: This ancient tool is perfect for grinding spices, herbs, and pastes, allowing you to unlock their full flavor potential.

2.12 Tips for Exploring Global Cuisine

Now that you have your ingredients and tools ready, here are some tips to help you make the most of your culinary exploration:

1. Research and Learn: Before diving into a specific cuisine, take some time to research its history, traditions, and iconic dishes.

Understanding the cultural context behind the cuisine will deepen your appreciation and enrich your cooking experience.

2. Start with Basic Recipes:
Begin your journey by trying simple and traditional recipes from each cuisine.

Mastering the foundational recipes will provide you with a solid understanding of the flavors and techniques unique to that cuisine.

3. Experiment with Flavors:
Don't be afraid to experiment and adapt recipes to suit your taste preferences.

While authenticity is important, feel free to add your own twist to dishes by incorporating local ingredients or personal touches.

4. Shop at Ethnic Markets:
Explore local ethnic markets or specialty stores to find authentic ingredients specific to the cuisine you're exploring.

These markets often carry a wide range of spices, condiments, and unique products that will elevate the authenticity of your dishes.

5. Engage with the Community: Join online forums, cooking groups, or social media communities where food enthusiasts share their experiences and recipes.

Engaging with like-minded individuals can provide valuable insights, recommendations, and inspiration.

6. Embrace Cooking Techniques: Different cuisines employ unique cooking techniques that contribute to their distinct flavors.

Experiment with stir-frying, braising, grilling, steaming, or slow-cooking to recreate authentic dishes and expand your culinary repertoire.

7. Take Notes and Document:
Keep a culinary journal to record your experiences, modifications, and new flavor combinations.

This will help you refine your recipes and preserve your culinary discoveries for future reference.

8. Plan International Dinner Parties:

Invite friends and family to experience the diverse flavors of global cuisine.

Hosting international dinner parties allows you to showcase your newfound culinary skills and share the joy of exploring different cultures through food.

9. Be Open-Minded and Adventurous:
Embrace the unfamiliar and be open to trying new ingredients, flavors, and textures.

A sense of adventure will enrich your culinary journey and open up a world of delicious possibilities.

Remember, exploring global cuisine is not just about cooking—it's a cultural experience that celebrates diversity and fosters a deeper connection with the world.

So, let your taste buds guide you, and enjoy every step of this flavorful adventure. Happy exploring!

3. European Delights

Europe is a continent known for its rich culinary traditions and diverse flavors.

 In this chapter, we will delve into some of the most iconic cuisines that have captivated taste buds around the world.

From the elegance of French cuisine to the comforting flavors of British pub fare, get ready to savor the delights that Europe has to offer.

3.11. Classic French Cuisine:

French cuisine is renowned for its sophistication and meticulous attention to detail.

From delicate pastries to exquisite sauces, French culinary traditions have influenced chefs worldwide.

Indulge in dishes such as Coq au Vin, Beef Bourguignon, Ratatouille, and Bouillabaisse.

Let's go:

i. Recipe: Coq au Vin

Ingredients:
- 4 chicken legs or 1 whole chicken, cut into pieces
- 4 slices of bacon, chopped
- 1 onion, diced
- 2 carrots, sliced
- 2 cloves of garlic, minced

- 8 ounces (225g) mushrooms, sliced
- 2 cups (480ml) red wine (such as Burgundy or Pinot Noir)
- 1 cup (240ml) chicken broth
- 2 tablespoons all-purpose flour
- 2 tablespoons butter
- 2 tablespoons fresh parsley, chopped
- Salt and pepper to taste

Instructions:
1. In a large Dutch oven or heavy-bottomed pot, cook the bacon over medium heat until crispy.

Remove the bacon from the pot and set aside, leaving the drippings in the pot.

2. Season the chicken pieces with salt and pepper. In the same pot with the bacon drippings, brown the chicken on all sides until golden brown.

Remove the chicken from the pot and set aside.

3. In the same pot, add the diced onion, sliced carrots, minced garlic, and sliced mushrooms.

Sauté for about 5 minutes, or until the vegetables are slightly softened.

4. Sprinkle the flour over the vegetables and stir well to coat.

Cook for another minute to cook off the raw flour taste.

5. Return the chicken and bacon to the pot.

Pour in the red wine and chicken broth.

Bring the mixture to a simmer, then cover and cook over low heat for about 1 to 1 ½ hours, or until the chicken is tender and cooked through.

6. Once the chicken is cooked, remove it from the pot and set aside.

Increase the heat to medium-high and let the sauce simmer for about 10 minutes, or until it has thickened slightly.

7. In a small bowl, mash together the butter and flour to create a smooth paste.

Gradually whisk the butter mixture into the sauce, stirring constantly until the sauce has thickened.

8. Return the chicken to the pot and simmer for another 5 minutes to allow the flavors to meld together.

9. Garnish with fresh parsley and serve hot with crusty bread or mashed potatoes.

Enjoy this classic French dish with its rich flavors and tender chicken, accompanied by a glass of red wine for a truly indulgent dining experience. Bon appétit!

ii. Recipe: Ratatouille

Ingredients:

- 1 eggplant, diced
- 1 zucchini, diced

- 1 yellow squash, diced
- 1 red bell pepper, diced
- 1 yellow bell pepper, diced
- 1 onion, diced
- 3 cloves of garlic, minced
- 2 tomatoes, diced
- 2 tablespoons tomato paste
- 2 tablespoons olive oil
- 1 teaspoon dried thyme
- 1 teaspoon dried oregano
- Salt and pepper to taste
- Fresh basil leaves, for garnish

Instructions:
1. Heat the olive oil in a large skillet or Dutch oven over medium heat.

Add the diced onion and minced garlic, and sauté until the onion is translucent and fragrant.

2. Add the diced eggplant, zucchini, yellow squash, red bell pepper, and yellow bell pepper to the skillet.

Stir well to combine with the onion and garlic.

Cook for about 5 minutes, or until the vegetables start to soften slightly.

3. Stir in the diced tomatoes, tomato paste, dried thyme, dried oregano, salt, and pepper.

Mix well to coat the vegetables with the tomato paste and herbs.

4. Reduce the heat to low, cover the skillet, and let the mixture simmer for about 30 minutes, stirring occasionally. This allows the flavors to meld together and the vegetables to become tender.

5. After 30 minutes, remove the lid and continue to cook for an additional 10 minutes to allow some of the excess liquid to evaporate and the ratatouille to thicken slightly.

6. Taste and adjust the seasoning if needed, adding more salt, pepper, or herbs to suit your taste preferences.

7. Remove from heat and let the ratatouille rest for a few minutes before serving. Garnish with fresh basil leaves for added freshness and aroma.

Ratatouille is a versatile dish that can be served as a side dish, a main course, or even as a filling for crepes or omelets.

Its vibrant colors and medley of flavors make it a true celebration of fresh summer vegetables.

 Enjoy this classic French recipe as a taste of Provence on your plate. Bon appétit!

iii. Recipe/ Dish: Bouillabaisse
   - Origin: France
   - Description: Bouillabaisse is a traditional Provençal fish stew originating from the coastal region of Marseille, France.

It is a flavorful and aromatic dish made with a variety of fish and shellfish, cooked in a broth infused with herbs, spices, and saffron.

Bouillabaisse typically includes fish such as red snapper, sea bass, and monkfish, along with shellfish like mussels, clams, and shrimp.

The broth is made with ingredients like tomatoes, onions, garlic, fennel, and a mix of herbs like thyme, bay leaf, and parsley.

The dish is known for its rich and complex flavors, and it is often served with a side of crusty bread and a rouille sauce, which is a garlic and saffron-infused mayonnaise.

Bouillabaisse is a beloved dish in French cuisine, showcasing the bountiful seafood of the Mediterranean region and reflecting the culinary traditions of the Provence area.

- Ingredients:
- Assorted fish (e.g., red snapper, sea bass, monkfish)
- Shellfish (e.g., mussels, clams, shrimp)
- Tomatoes
- Onions
- Garlic
- Fennel
- Olive oil
- White wine
- Saffron
- Thyme
- Bay leaf
- Parsley
- Crusty bread (for serving)
- Rouille sauce (for serving)

- Instructions:
1. Heat olive oil in a large pot over medium heat. Add onions, garlic, and fennel, and sauté until softened.

2. Add tomatoes, white wine, saffron, thyme, and bay leaf to the pot. Stir well and bring to a simmer.

3. Add the assorted fish and shellfish to the pot, arranging them in a single layer. Cover and cook for a few minutes until the fish starts to cook through.

4. Gently stir the ingredients in the pot, ensuring they are well submerged in the broth. Cover and continue to cook until the fish is fully cooked and the shellfish have opened.

5. Remove from heat and sprinkle with chopped parsley.

6. Serve the bouillabaisse in bowls, along with crusty bread and rouille sauce on the side.

7. Enjoy this delightful French seafood stew, savoring the flavors of the Mediterranean and the rich broth that characterizes bouillabaisse.

Discover the art of baking with recipes like Croissants, Tarte Tatin, and Crème Brûlée.

Unleash your inner chef as you master the techniques of sautéing, braising, and creating the perfect emulsion.

i. Recipe/Dish: Croissants

- Origin: France

- Description: Croissants are flaky, buttery pastries that have become synonymous with French cuisine.

Originating from France, croissants are a staple of French bakeries and breakfast tables around the world.

These crescent-shaped pastries are made with a laminated dough, which consists of alternating layers of butter and dough.

The dough is rolled, folded, and shaped into triangles before being baked to golden perfection.

The result is a light, airy pastry with a crispy exterior and a soft, buttery interior.

Croissants can be enjoyed plain or filled with various sweet or savory fillings such as chocolate, almond paste, or ham and cheese.

They are often enjoyed alongside a cup of coffee or tea and are a beloved breakfast or brunch treat.

- **Ingredients:**
  - All-purpose flour
  - Unsalted butter
  - Sugar
  - Salt
  - Active dry yeast
  - Milk
  - Water

- **Instructions:**
  1. In a mixing bowl, combine flour, sugar, salt, and yeast.

  2. Add milk and water to the dry ingredients and mix until a dough forms.

  3. Knead the dough on a lightly floured surface until it becomes smooth and elastic.

  4. Roll out the dough into a rectangle and spread softened butter over two-thirds of the dough.

  5. Fold the unbuttered third of the dough over the buttered section, then fold the remaining buttered third over the folded portion.

6. Rotate the dough 90 degrees and repeat the rolling and folding process.

7. Repeat this process a few more times, chilling the dough between each fold.

8. Roll out the dough into a large rectangle and cut it into triangles.

9. Roll each triangle tightly from the wider end towards the tip, shaping it into a crescent.

10. Place the croissants on a baking sheet and let them rise until doubled in size.

11. Preheat the oven and brush the croissants with an egg wash for a shiny finish.

12. Bake the croissants until golden brown and flaky.

13. Remove from the oven and allow them to cool slightly before serving.

14. Enjoy these delicious, buttery croissants as a delightful breakfast or anytime treat.

ii. Recipe: Tarte Tatin

Ingredients:
- 6-8 medium-sized apples, peeled, cored, and halved
- 1 cup (200g) granulated sugar
- 1/2 cup (113g) unsalted butter
- 1 teaspoon vanilla extract
- 1 sheet of puff pastry, thawed if frozen
- Whipped cream or vanilla ice cream, for serving (optional)

Instructions:
1. Preheat your oven to 375°F (190°C).

2. In an oven-safe skillet or Tarte Tatin dish, melt the butter over medium heat.

Sprinkle the sugar evenly over the melted butter and let it cook, stirring occasionally, until the sugar dissolves and turns amber in color, about 5-7 minutes.

Be careful not to burn the caramel.

3. Remove the skillet from heat and carefully arrange the apple halves, round side down, in the caramel.

Pack them tightly together in a circular pattern, filling the entire skillet.

4. Return the skillet to medium heat and cook the apples in the caramel for an additional 10-12 minutes, allowing the apples to soften slightly and absorb the caramel flavors.

Gently press the apples down with a spatula to ensure they are evenly coated with the caramel.

5. While the apples are cooking, roll out the puff pastry sheet on a lightly floured surface until it is slightly larger than the skillet.

Prick the surface of the pastry with a fork to prevent it from puffing too much during baking.

6. Carefully place the puff pastry over the apples, tucking in the edges around the apples to create a seal.

7. Transfer the skillet to the preheated oven and bake for 25-30 minutes, or until the pastry is golden brown and crispy.

8. Remove the skillet from the oven and let it cool for 5 minutes.

Place a serving platter or plate on top of the skillet, then carefully and quickly invert the Tarte Tatin onto the platter, using oven mitts or towels to protect your hands.

9. Serve the Tarte Tatin warm, either on its own or accompanied by whipped cream or vanilla ice cream for a delightful contrast of flavors.

Slice and enjoy the delicious caramelized apples and buttery pastry.

The Tarte Tatin is a classic French dessert that combines the simplicity of caramelized apples with the elegance of puff pastry.

Its upside-down presentation and rich flavors make it a showstopper on any dessert table. Indulge in this delectable treat and savor the sweet taste of French culinary tradition. Bon appétit!

iii. Dish: Crème Brûlée

  - Origin: France

  - Description: Crème brûlée is a classic French dessert known for its rich and creamy texture, contrasting with a crisp caramelized sugar topping.

This elegant dessert consists of a smooth custard base made from a mixture of cream, egg yolks, sugar, and vanilla.

The custard is baked until set, then chilled to create a silky and velvety consistency.

Just before serving, a layer of sugar is sprinkled on top and caramelized with a kitchen torch or broiler, forming a delicate and crunchy caramelized crust.

The combination of the creamy custard and the brittle caramelized sugar creates a delightful contrast in both taste and texture.

Crème brûlée is often served in individual ramekins and is a popular dessert choice in fine dining establishments around the world.

- **Ingredients:**
  - Heavy cream
  - Granulated sugar
  - Egg yolks
  - Vanilla extract

- **Instructions:**
  1. Preheat the oven and prepare a baking dish filled with hot water for a water bath.

  2. In a saucepan, heat the cream until it begins to simmer. Remove from heat.

  3. In a separate bowl, whisk together the sugar and egg yolks until well combined.

  4. Slowly pour the heated cream into the egg mixture while whisking continuously.

  5. Stir in the vanilla extract and mix until the custard is smooth and homogeneous.

  6. Strain the custard mixture through a fine mesh sieve to remove any lumps.

  7. Divide the custard among ramekins or oven-safe dishes.

8. Place the ramekins in the prepared baking dish with hot water, ensuring the water reaches halfway up the sides of the ramekins.

9. Carefully transfer the baking dish to the preheated oven and bake until the custard is set around the edges but still slightly jiggly in the center.

10. Remove the ramekins from the water bath and let them cool to room temperature.

11. Once cooled, refrigerate the custards for at least 2 hours, or until thoroughly chilled.

12. Just before serving, sprinkle a thin layer of granulated sugar on top of each custard.

13. Caramelize the sugar using a kitchen torch or by placing the ramekins under a broiler until the sugar melts and forms a golden crust.

14. Allow the caramelized sugar to harden for a few minutes, then serve the crème brûlée immediately.

15. Enjoy the creamy, caramelized goodness of this classic French dessert.

3.12. Italian Pasta and Pizza:

Italian cuisine holds a special place in the hearts of food lovers everywhere.

Dive into the world of pasta and experience the joy of preparing homemade Tagliatelle, Lasagna, or Ravioli.

i. Recipe: Tagliatelle with Mushroom Sauce

Ingredients:
- 8 ounces (225g) tagliatelle pasta
- 8 ounces (225g) mushrooms (such as cremini or button), sliced
- 2 tablespoons olive oil
- 2 cloves of garlic, minced
- 1/4 cup (60ml) dry white wine
- 1 cup (240ml) heavy cream
- 1/4 cup (25g) grated Parmesan cheese
- 2 tablespoons chopped fresh parsley
- Salt and pepper, to taste

Instructions:
1. Bring a large pot of salted water to a boil.

Cook the tagliatelle pasta according to the package instructions until al dente.

Drain the pasta and set aside.

2. While the pasta is cooking, heat the olive oil in a large skillet over medium heat.

Add the sliced mushrooms to the skillet and cook until they release their moisture and start to brown, about 5-7 minutes.

3. Add the minced garlic to the skillet and sauté for another minute until fragrant.

4. Pour in the white wine and cook for a couple of minutes, allowing the alcohol to evaporate.

5. Reduce the heat to low and stir in the heavy cream.

Simmer the sauce gently for a few minutes, stirring occasionally, until it thickens slightly.

6. Add the grated Parmesan cheese to the sauce and stir until melted and well combined.

Season with salt and pepper to taste.

7. Return the cooked and drained tagliatelle to the skillet with the mushroom sauce.

Toss the pasta in the sauce until it is evenly coated.

8. Sprinkle the chopped fresh parsley over the pasta and give it a final toss to incorporate the parsley.

9. Serve the tagliatelle with mushroom sauce immediately, garnished with additional Parmesan cheese and a sprinkle of fresh parsley if desired.

Enjoy this comforting and flavorful pasta dish that showcases the earthy goodness of mushrooms.

Buon appetito!

ii. Recipe: Classic Lasagna

Ingredients:
- 12 lasagna noodles
- 1 pound (450g) ground beef
- 1/2 pound (225g) Italian sausage
- 1 onion, diced
- 3 cloves of garlic, minced
- 1 can (28 ounces/800g) crushed tomatoes
- 1 can (6 ounces/170g) tomato paste

- 2 teaspoons dried basil
- 2 teaspoons dried oregano
- 1 teaspoon sugar
- 1/2 teaspoon salt
- 1/4 teaspoon black pepper
- 2 cups (450g) ricotta cheese
- 2 cups (225g) shredded mozzarella cheese
- 1/2 cup (50g) grated Parmesan cheese
- Fresh basil leaves, for garnish (optional)

Instructions:
1. Preheat your oven to 375°F (190°C).

2. Cook the lasagna noodles according to the package instructions until al dente.

Drain the noodles and set them aside.

3. In a large skillet, brown the ground beef and Italian sausage over medium heat, breaking it up into crumbles with a spatula or wooden spoon.

Once cooked, remove any excess grease from the skillet.

4. Add the diced onion and minced garlic to the skillet with the cooked meat.

Sauté until the onion becomes translucent and the garlic is fragrant.

5. Stir in the crushed tomatoes, tomato paste, dried basil, dried oregano, sugar, salt, and black pepper.

Simmer the sauce for about 15-20 minutes to allow the flavors to meld together.

6. In a separate bowl, combine the ricotta cheese and shredded mozzarella cheese.

Mix well until evenly blended.

7. Assemble the lasagna by spreading a thin layer of the meat sauce on the bottom of a 9x13-inch (23x33cm) baking dish.

Arrange a layer of cooked lasagna noodles over the sauce, slightly overlapping them.

8. Spread a layer of the ricotta and mozzarella cheese mixture over the noodles, followed by another layer of the meat sauce.

Repeat the layers, finishing with a layer of meat sauce on top.

9. Sprinkle the grated Parmesan cheese evenly over the top layer of meat sauce.

10. Cover the baking dish with aluminum foil and bake in the preheated oven for 30 minutes.

Then, remove the foil and continue baking for an additional 15 minutes, or until the lasagna is hot and bubbly, and the cheese on top is golden brown.

11. Remove the lasagna from the oven and let it cool for a few minutes before serving.

Garnish with fresh basil leaves if desired.

12. Slice the lasagna into portions and serve it warm.

This classic lasagna is a hearty and satisfying dish that brings together layers of pasta, meat sauce, and cheesy goodness.

Enjoy the comforting flavors of this Italian favorite.

Buon appetito!

iii. Recipe: Spinach and Ricotta Ravioli

Ingredients:
For the pasta dough:
- 2 cups (250g) all-purpose flour
- 3 large eggs
- 1/2 teaspoon salt

For the filling:
- 1 cup (225g) ricotta cheese
- 1 cup (60g) fresh spinach, cooked and squeezed dry
- 1/4 cup (25g) grated Parmesan cheese
- 1/4 teaspoon nutmeg
- Salt and pepper, to taste

For the sauce:
- 4 tablespoons unsalted butter
- 2 cloves of garlic, minced
- Fresh sage leaves, for garnish
- Grated Parmesan cheese, for serving

Instructions:
1. To make the pasta dough, place the flour on a clean surface and make a well in the center.

Crack the eggs into the well and add the salt.

Using a fork, gradually beat the eggs and incorporate the flour until a dough forms.

2. Knead the dough for about 5-7 minutes, until it becomes smooth and elastic.

Wrap the dough in plastic wrap and let it rest at room temperature for 30 minutes.

3. Meanwhile, prepare the filling by combining the ricotta cheese, cooked spinach, grated Parmesan cheese, nutmeg, salt, and pepper in a bowl.

Mix well until all the ingredients are evenly incorporated.

4. After the dough has rested, divide it into smaller portions.

Roll out one portion at a time on a floured surface until it is thin and translucent.

Keep the remaining dough covered to prevent it from drying out.

5. Place teaspoon-sized dollops of the filling evenly spaced on one half of the rolled-out dough.

 Fold the other half of the dough over the filling, pressing down gently to seal the edges.

6. Use a knife or a ravioli cutter to cut the ravioli into individual pieces. Press the edges with a fork to ensure a tight seal.

7. Bring a large pot of salted water to a boil.

Carefully drop the ravioli into the boiling water and cook for about 3-4 minutes, or until they float to the surface.

 Remove the cooked ravioli with a slotted spoon and set them aside.

8. In a separate skillet, melt the butter over medium heat.

 Add the minced garlic and sauté until fragrant, about 1-2 minutes. Remove from heat.

9. Place the cooked ravioli in the skillet with the garlic butter and gently toss to coat them with the sauce.

10. Serve the spinach and ricotta ravioli on individual plates, garnished with fresh sage leaves.

Sprinkle grated Parmesan cheese on top for an extra burst of flavor.

11. Enjoy the delicate and delicious spinach and ricotta ravioli as a delightful pasta dish that showcases the flavors of homemade Italian cuisine.

Buon appetito!

Learn the secrets of crafting the perfect pizza, from preparing the dough to creating mouthwatering toppings like Margherita, Quattro Formaggi, or Prosciutto e Funghi.

Pizza is a beloved dish that has captured the hearts (and taste buds) of people all over the world.

From its humble origins in Naples, Italy, pizza has become a global sensation with countless variations and flavors.

While enjoying a slice of pizza is always a pleasure, there is something truly special about crafting your own homemade pizza.

We will now unveil the secrets to creating the perfect pizza, starting with the foundation of any great pie—the dough—and exploring mouthwatering toppings such as the classic Margherita, indulgent Quattro Formaggi, and savory Prosciutto e Funghi.

1. Mastering the Dough:

a. Selecting the right flour:
The type of flour you use greatly impacts the texture and flavor of the pizza dough.

Opt for high-quality Italian "00" flour for an authentic Neapolitan-style pizza, or experiment with other flours like bread flour or a blend of whole wheat and all-purpose flour for a different taste and texture.

b. Proper kneading:
Kneading the dough thoroughly helps develop gluten strands, resulting in a light and airy crust.

Give the dough enough time to rise and rest, allowing the flavors to develop and the gluten to relax.

c. Achieving the right consistency:
The dough should be soft, smooth, and slightly sticky. Add water or flour as needed during the mixing process to achieve the perfect consistency.

2. Sauce and Cheese:

a. Simplicity is key:
A good pizza sauce should be made from ripe tomatoes, preferably San Marzano, blended with a touch of olive oil, garlic, salt, and a sprinkle of dried oregano.

Strive for a balanced flavor that complements the toppings without overpowering them.

b. Fresh mozzarella:

Opt for fresh mozzarella cheese, preferably buffalo mozzarella, for its creamy texture and mild flavor.

Tear or slice it into small pieces and distribute it evenly across the pizza for gooey and melty goodness.

3. Classic Margherita:
a. Celebrating simplicity:
The Margherita pizza is a true classic that showcases the essence of Italian pizza.

Use fresh basil leaves, sliced tomatoes, and mozzarella cheese to create a tricolor masterpiece that represents the Italian flag.

b. A touch of olive oil:
Drizzle a little extra-virgin olive oil over the pizza just before baking to enhance the flavors and add a touch of richness.

Recipe: Classic Margherita Pizza

Ingredients:
- 1 pound (450g) pizza dough
- 1/2 cup pizza sauce
- 8 ounces (225g) fresh mozzarella cheese, torn or sliced
- 2-3 ripe tomatoes, thinly sliced
- Fresh basil leaves, torn
- Extra-virgin olive oil, for drizzling
- Salt and pepper, to taste

Instructions:
1. Preheat your oven to the highest temperature it can reach (usually around 500°F or 260°C). If you have a pizza stone, place it in the oven while it preheats.

2. On a floured surface, roll out the pizza dough into a thin round or your desired shape. Transfer the dough to a parchment-lined baking sheet or a pizza peel if using a stone.

3. Spread a thin layer of pizza sauce evenly over the dough, leaving a small border around the edges.

4. Distribute the torn or sliced fresh mozzarella cheese over the sauce, covering the pizza evenly.

5. Arrange the thinly sliced tomatoes on top of the cheese, overlapping them slightly. Sprinkle a pinch of salt and pepper over the tomatoes.

6. Slide the pizza onto the preheated baking stone or place the baking sheet in the oven.

7. Bake the pizza for about 10-15 minutes or until the crust is golden brown and the cheese is bubbly and slightly browned.

8. Remove the pizza from the oven and immediately sprinkle torn fresh basil leaves over the top.

9. Drizzle a generous amount of extra-virgin olive oil over the pizza, allowing it to soak into the toppings and crust.

10. Let the pizza cool for a few minutes before slicing it into wedges or squares.

11. Serve the classic Margherita pizza as a delicious and flavorful homage to the simplicity of Italian cuisine.

Enjoy the harmony of tangy tomatoes, creamy mozzarella, fragrant basil, and the crispness of the crust.

 Buon appetito!

4. Quattro Formaggi:
a. A cheese lover's dream:
This pizza is a celebration of cheese with a delightful blend of four different varieties.

Combine mozzarella, Gorgonzola, Parmesan, and fontina cheeses for a flavor explosion that will satisfy any cheese lover's cravings.

b. Balance the flavors:
While the cheese takes center stage, balance the richness with a drizzle of honey or a handful of arugula to add a touch of sweetness and freshness.

Recipe: Quattro Formaggi Pizza

Ingredients:
- 1 pound (450g) pizza dough
- 1/2 cup pizza sauce
- 4 ounces (115g) fresh mozzarella cheese, torn or sliced
- 4 ounces (115g) Gorgonzola cheese, crumbled
- 4 ounces (115g) Parmesan cheese, grated
- 4 ounces (115g) fontina cheese, shredded
- Honey, for drizzling (optional)
- Fresh arugula, for garnish (optional)

Instructions:
1. Preheat your oven to the highest temperature it can reach (usually around 500°F or 260°C).

If you have a pizza stone, place it in the oven while it preheats.

2. On a floured surface, roll out the pizza dough into a thin round or your desired shape.

Transfer the dough to a parchment-lined baking sheet or a pizza peel if using a stone.

3. Spread a thin layer of pizza sauce evenly over the dough, leaving a small border around the edges.

4. Sprinkle the torn or sliced fresh mozzarella cheese over the sauce, covering the pizza evenly.

5. Crumble the Gorgonzola cheese over the mozzarella, distributing it evenly across the pizza.

6. Sprinkle the grated Parmesan cheese over the other cheeses, ensuring it is evenly spread.

7. Finish by spreading the shredded fontina cheese over the top, ensuring all the cheeses are evenly distributed.

8. Slide the pizza onto the preheated baking stone or place the baking sheet in the oven.

9. Bake the pizza for about 10-15 minutes or until the crust is golden brown and the cheese is melted and bubbly.

10. Remove the pizza from the oven and let it cool for a few minutes.

11. If desired, drizzle a touch of honey over the hot pizza to add a subtle sweetness that balances the richness of the cheeses.

12. Garnish with fresh arugula leaves for a refreshing and peppery contrast.

13. Slice the Quattro Formaggi pizza into wedges or squares and serve it as a decadent and indulgent treat.

Enjoy the harmonious combination of four delicious cheeses and the contrasting flavors of honey and arugula.

Buon appetito!

5. Prosciutto e Funghi:
a. The perfect duo:
Prosciutto (thinly sliced Italian cured ham) and mushrooms create a flavor combination that is hard to resist.

Layer prosciutto and sautéed mushrooms over the pizza, and sprinkle with grated Parmesan cheese for an indulgent treat.

b. Enhance the aroma:
Add a sprinkle of dried thyme or fresh rosemary to infuse the pizza with a fragrant herbal note that complements the earthiness of the mushrooms and the saltiness of the prosciutto.

Recipe: Prosciutto e Funghi Pizza

Ingredients:
- 1 pound (450g) pizza dough
- 1/2 cup pizza sauce
- 8 ounces (225g) fresh mozzarella cheese, torn or sliced
- 4 ounces (115g) sliced prosciutto
- 4 ounces (115g) mushrooms, sliced
- 1/4 cup grated Parmesan cheese
- Dried thyme or fresh rosemary, for garnish
- Olive oil, for drizzling

Instructions:
1. Preheat your oven to the highest temperature it can reach (usually around 500°F or 260°C). If you have a pizza stone, place it in the oven while it preheats.

2. On a floured surface, roll out the pizza dough into a thin round or your desired shape. Transfer the dough to a parchment-lined baking sheet or a pizza peel if using a stone.

3. Spread a thin layer of pizza sauce evenly over the dough, leaving a small border around the edges.

4. Distribute the torn or sliced fresh mozzarella cheese over the sauce, ensuring it is evenly spread.

5. Arrange the slices of prosciutto over the cheese, evenly covering the pizza.

6. Scatter the sliced mushrooms over the prosciutto, distributing them evenly.

7. Sprinkle the grated Parmesan cheese over the toppings, ensuring it is evenly spread.

8. Garnish the pizza with a sprinkle of dried thyme or fresh rosemary for added aroma.

9. Slide the pizza onto the preheated baking stone or place the baking sheet in the oven.

10. Bake the pizza for about 10-15 minutes or until the crust is golden brown and the cheese is melted and slightly browned.

11. Remove the pizza from the oven and let it cool for a few minutes.

12. Drizzle a touch of olive oil over the hot pizza to enhance the flavors and add a glossy finish.

13. Slice the Prosciutto e Funghi pizza into wedges or squares and serve it as a delightful combination of salty prosciutto, earthy mushrooms, and savory cheeses.

Enjoy the wonderful blend of flavors and textures in each bite.

Buon appetito!

Conclusion:
Crafting the perfect pizza is a culinary journey that combines the art of dough-making, sauce creation, and the selection of tantalizing toppings.

Discover the simplicity of Italian flavors with dishes like Caprese Salad, Osso Buco, and Tiramisu.

i. Recipe: Caprese Salad

Ingredients:
- 4 ripe tomatoes
- 8 ounces (225g) fresh mozzarella cheese
- Fresh basil leaves
- Extra-virgin olive oil
- Balsamic glaze (optional)
- Salt and pepper, to taste

Instructions:
1. Slice the tomatoes and fresh mozzarella cheese into equal-sized, round slices, approximately 1/4-inch thick.

2. Arrange the tomato slices on a serving platter or individual plates.

3. Place a slice of fresh mozzarella cheese on top of each tomato slice.

4. Take the fresh basil leaves and tear them into smaller pieces.

 Scatter the torn basil leaves over the tomatoes and mozzarella.

5. Drizzle a generous amount of extra-virgin olive oil over the salad, ensuring it coats the ingredients.

6. If desired, drizzle balsamic glaze over the salad to add a tangy and slightly sweet flavor.

This step is optional but enhances the traditional Caprese salad.

7. Season the salad with salt and pepper to taste.

8. Allow the flavors to meld together for a few minutes before serving to allow the tomatoes and mozzarella to absorb the flavors of the basil, olive oil, and seasonings.

9. Serve the Caprese salad as a refreshing and vibrant appetizer or side dish.

 It beautifully combines the freshness of ripe tomatoes, the creaminess of fresh mozzarella, and the aromatic touch of basil.

Enjoy the simplicity and elegance of this classic Italian dish.

Buon appetito!

ii. Recipe: Osso Buco

Ingredients:
- 4 veal shanks, about 1 1/2 inches thick

- Salt and pepper, to taste
- All-purpose flour, for dredging
- 3 tablespoons olive oil
- 1 onion, finely chopped
- 2 carrots, finely chopped
- 2 celery stalks, finely chopped
- 4 cloves garlic, minced
- 1 cup dry white wine
- 1 can (14 ounces) diced tomatoes
- 1 cup beef or veal broth
- 1 tablespoon tomato paste
- 1 bay leaf
- 1 teaspoon dried thyme
- Gremolata for garnish:
  - Zest of 1 lemon
  - 2 cloves garlic, minced
  - 2 tablespoons fresh parsley, finely chopped

Instructions:
1. Season the veal shanks generously with salt and pepper. Dredge them in flour, shaking off any excess.

2. In a large, heavy-bottomed pot or Dutch oven, heat the olive oil over medium-high heat.

3. Brown the veal shanks on all sides until they develop a rich golden color. Remove the shanks from the pot and set them aside.

4. In the same pot, add the chopped onion, carrots, celery, and minced garlic.

Sauté the vegetables until they become soft and lightly golden.

5. Pour in the white wine and deglaze the pot, scraping up any browned bits from the bottom.

6. Add the diced tomatoes, beef or veal broth, tomato paste, bay leaf, and dried thyme to the pot.

Stir well to combine the ingredients.

7. Return the veal shanks to the pot, nestling them into the liquid and vegetables.

8. Bring the mixture to a simmer, then reduce the heat to low.

Cover the pot and let the osso buco gently simmer for about 2 to 2 1/2 hours, or until the meat becomes tender and begins to pull away from the bone.

9. While the osso buco cooks, prepare the gremolata.

In a small bowl, combine the lemon zest, minced garlic, and finely chopped parsley. Mix well and set aside.

10. Once the osso buco is cooked and tender, remove the bay leaf from the pot.

Taste the sauce and adjust the seasoning with salt and pepper, if needed.

11. Serve the osso buco hot, placing each veal shank on a plate.

Spoon some of the flavorful sauce and vegetables over the meat.

12. Garnish each serving with a sprinkle of the prepared gremolata, adding a vibrant and aromatic touch to the dish.

13. Osso buco is traditionally served with risotto or creamy polenta, providing a perfect accompaniment to soak up the delicious sauce.

14. Enjoy the rich and tender veal shanks, infused with the flavors of the aromatic vegetables and savory sauce.

Osso buco is a comforting and satisfying dish that showcases the beauty of slow-cooked meat.

Buon appetito!

iii. Recipe: Tiramisu

Ingredients:
- 6 egg yolks
- 3/4 cup granulated sugar
- 2/3 cup milk
- 1 1/4 cups heavy cream
- 8 ounces mascarpone cheese
- 1 teaspoon vanilla extract
- 1 cup strong brewed coffee, cooled
- 2 tablespoons coffee liqueur (such as Kahlua or Tia Maria)
- 24 ladyfingers
- Unsweetened cocoa powder, for dusting

Instructions:
1. In a heatproof bowl, whisk together the egg yolks and sugar until well combined.

2. Place the bowl over a saucepan of simmering water, making sure the bottom of the bowl does not touch the water. Whisk constantly for about 5 minutes or until the mixture becomes thick and pale yellow in color.

3. Remove the bowl from the heat and whisk in the milk. Let the mixture cool to room temperature.

4. In a separate bowl, beat the heavy cream until stiff peaks form.

5. In another bowl, whisk the mascarpone cheese and vanilla extract until smooth and creamy.

6. Gently fold the whipped cream into the mascarpone mixture until well combined.

7. In a shallow dish, combine the cooled brewed coffee and coffee liqueur.

8. Dip each ladyfinger into the coffee mixture, allowing them to soak briefly on each side. Be careful not to oversoak them, as they may become too soft.

9. Line the bottom of a rectangular serving dish or individual dessert cups with half of the soaked ladyfingers.

10. Spread half of the mascarpone cream mixture over the ladyfingers, ensuring an even layer.

11. Repeat the layers with the remaining soaked ladyfingers and mascarpone cream.

12. Cover the dish with plastic wrap and refrigerate for at least 4 hours or overnight to allow the flavors to meld and the dessert to set.

13. Just before serving, dust the top of the tiramisu with a generous amount of unsweetened cocoa powder using a fine-mesh sieve.

14. Cut into slices or spoon into individual servings and serve chilled.

15. Tiramisu is a classic Italian dessert known for its creamy, coffee-infused layers.

 Enjoy the delicate balance of flavors and textures, from the soaked ladyfingers to the rich mascarpone cream.

Buon appetito! :

3.13. Spanish Tapas and Paella:

Spanish cuisine is known for its vibrant colors, bold flavors, and communal dining experiences. Explore the world of tapas, small plates bursting with flavor.

Let's prepare classics like Patatas Bravas, Gambas al Ajillo, and Tortilla Española.

i. Recipe: Patatas Bravas

Ingredients:
- 2 pounds (900g) potatoes, peeled and cut into 1-inch cubes
- Vegetable oil, for frying
- Salt, to taste
- 1/2 cup tomato sauce
- 2 tablespoons mayonnaise
- 1 tablespoon hot sauce (such as Tabasco or Sriracha)
- 1 teaspoon smoked paprika
- 1/2 teaspoon garlic powder
- Fresh parsley, chopped (for garnish)

Instructions:
1. Rinse the potato cubes under cold water to remove any excess starch. Pat them dry with a clean kitchen towel.

2. In a large skillet or deep-fryer, heat enough vegetable oil to fully submerge the potato cubes.

Heat the oil to around 350°F (175°C).

3. Carefully add the potato cubes to the hot oil, working in batches if necessary to avoid overcrowding the skillet.

Fry the potatoes for about 6-8 minutes or until they become golden and crispy.

Stir occasionally to ensure even cooking.

4. Using a slotted spoon or a spider strainer, remove the fried potatoes from the oil and transfer them to a paper towel-lined plate to drain excess oil.

Season the potatoes with salt while they are still hot.

5. In a small bowl, combine the tomato sauce, mayonnaise, hot sauce, smoked paprika, and garlic powder.

Stir well to create a smooth and spicy sauce.

6. Arrange the fried potato cubes on a serving platter or individual plates.

7. Drizzle the spicy tomato sauce over the potatoes, ensuring they are coated evenly.

8. Garnish with fresh chopped parsley for a pop of color and freshness.

9. Serve the Patatas Bravas as a delightful and flavorful appetizer or side dish.

These crispy fried potatoes paired with the zesty and tangy sauce create a delicious combination of textures and flavors.

Enjoy the bold taste of this popular Spanish dish.

Buen provecho!

ii. Recipe: Gambas al Ajillo (Garlic Shrimp)

Ingredients:
- 1 pound (450g) large shrimp, peeled and deveined
- 4 tablespoons olive oil
- 6 cloves garlic, minced
- 1/2 teaspoon red pepper flakes (optional, for heat)
- 2 tablespoons chopped fresh parsley
- Salt, to taste
- Lemon wedges, for serving

Instructions:
1. Heat the olive oil in a large skillet over medium heat.

2. Add the minced garlic and red pepper flakes (if using) to the skillet.

Sauté for about 1 minute until the garlic becomes fragrant but not browned.

3. Increase the heat to medium-high and add the shrimp to the skillet.

Cook the shrimp for about 2-3 minutes per side until they turn pink and opaque.

4. Stir in the chopped fresh parsley and season with salt to taste.

Toss the shrimp in the garlic and parsley mixture to ensure they are well-coated.

5. Remove the skillet from the heat and let the flavors meld for a minute or two.

6. Transfer the Gambas al Ajillo to a serving dish or individual plates.

7. Serve the garlic shrimp hot, garnished with fresh parsley and accompanied by lemon wedges.

8. Squeeze the lemon wedges over the shrimp just before eating to add a tangy and bright flavor.

9. Gambas al Ajillo is a popular Spanish tapas dish known for its simplicity and bold flavors.

Enjoy the succulent shrimp infused with the aromatic garlic and herbs. It pairs well with crusty bread or can be served as part of a tapas spread.

Buen provecho!

iii. Recipe: Tortilla Española (Spanish Omelette)

Ingredients:
- 4 medium potatoes
- 1 onion
- 6 large eggs
- 1/4 cup olive oil
- Salt, to taste
- Freshly ground black pepper, to taste
- Fresh parsley, chopped (for garnish)

Instructions:
1. Peel the potatoes and slice them into thin rounds.

Finely chop the onion.

2. In a large non-stick skillet, heat the olive oil over medium heat.

3. Add the sliced potatoes and chopped onion to the skillet.

Cook them gently, stirring occasionally, until the potatoes are tender but not browned.

This process may take around 15 minutes. Make sure to adjust the heat if needed to prevent browning.

4. While the potatoes and onion are cooking, crack the eggs into a large bowl.

Season them with salt and freshly ground black pepper. Whisk the eggs until well beaten.

5. Using a slotted spoon, transfer the cooked potatoes and onion to the bowl with the beaten eggs.

Stir gently to combine, ensuring the potatoes and onion are evenly coated with the eggs.

6. Discard any excess oil from the skillet, leaving just a thin coating.

7. Return the skillet to medium heat and pour the potato and egg mixture back into the pan.

Use a spatula to spread it out evenly.

8. Cook the tortilla for about 4-5 minutes, or until the edges start to set and the bottom is golden brown.

Shake the pan occasionally to prevent sticking.

9. To flip the tortilla, place a large plate upside down on top of the skillet.

Hold the plate firmly against the skillet and carefully invert it, allowing the tortilla to slide onto the plate.

10. Slide the tortilla back into the skillet, uncooked side down.

Continue cooking for another 4-5 minutes, or until the center is set and the tortilla is cooked through.

11. Once cooked, transfer the tortilla to a cutting board or serving plate. Let it cool slightly before slicing.

12. Garnish the Tortilla Española with freshly chopped parsley.

13. Serve the Spanish omelette warm or at room temperature, either as a main course or a delightful tapas dish.

Enjoy the combination of creamy potatoes, tender onion, and fluffy eggs in every delicious bite.

Buen provecho!

Immerse yourself in the art of making traditional Paella, combining saffron-infused rice with an array of ingredients such as seafood, chicken, or vegetables.

Recipe: Paella

Ingredients:
- 2 cups Arborio rice (or short-grain rice)
- 4 cups chicken or vegetable broth

- 1 pound boneless, skinless chicken thighs, cut into bite-sized pieces
- 1/2 pound chorizo sausage, sliced
- 1 large onion, finely chopped
- 4 cloves garlic, minced
- 1 red bell pepper, sliced
- 1 yellow bell pepper, sliced
- 1 cup diced tomatoes
- 1 teaspoon smoked paprika
- 1/2 teaspoon saffron threads
- 1/2 teaspoon turmeric
- 1 cup fresh or frozen peas
- 1 pound large shrimp, peeled and deveined
- 1/2 cup pitted green olives
- Fresh parsley, chopped (for garnish)
- Lemon wedges, for serving
- Olive oil, for cooking
- Salt and pepper, to taste

Instructions:

1. In a large paella pan or a wide, shallow skillet, heat olive oil over medium heat.

2. Add the chicken pieces to the pan and cook until browned on all sides.

Remove the chicken from the pan and set it aside.

3. In the same pan, add the sliced chorizo and cook until it starts to release its oils and becomes slightly crispy.

 Remove the chorizo from the pan and set it aside.

4. Add more olive oil to the pan if needed.

Sauté the chopped onion and minced garlic until they become translucent and fragrant.

5. Stir in the sliced red and yellow bell peppers, and cook for a few minutes until they begin to soften.

6. Add the diced tomatoes, smoked paprika, saffron threads, and turmeric to the pan.

Stir well to combine the ingredients and let them cook for a minute to release their flavors.

7. Add the Arborio rice to the pan and stir it to coat it evenly with the spices and vegetables.

8. Pour in the chicken or vegetable broth and bring the mixture to a simmer.

Reduce the heat to low and let the rice cook uncovered for about 10-15 minutes, stirring occasionally.

9. Once the rice has absorbed most of the liquid, arrange the cooked chicken, chorizo slices, and peas on top.

Gently press them into the rice.

10. Place the shrimp and green olives on the rice, pressing them slightly into the mixture.

11. Cover the pan with a lid or aluminum foil and let the paella cook for an additional 10-15 minutes, or until the rice is tender and the shrimp are cooked through.

12. Remove the lid and let the paella rest for a few minutes before serving.

13. Garnish the paella with fresh chopped parsley and serve it with lemon wedges on the side.

14. Enjoy this vibrant and flavorful Spanish dish that brings together a medley of ingredients and tastes.

The combination of saffron-infused rice, tender chicken and shrimp, smoky chorizo, and colorful vegetables is sure to impress.

Serve it as the centerpiece of your meal and savor the rich flavors of paella.

Buen provecho!

Don't forget to indulge in the sweetness of Churros con Chocolate or Crema Catalana for a delightful ending to your Spanish culinary adventure.

i. Recipe: Churros con Chocolate

Ingredients:
For the churros:
- 1 cup water
- 2 tablespoons sugar
- 1/2 teaspoon salt
- 2 tablespoons vegetable oil
- 1 cup all-purpose flour
- Vegetable oil, for frying

For the chocolate dipping sauce:
- 4 ounces dark chocolate, finely chopped
- 1 cup milk
- 2 tablespoons sugar
- 1/2 teaspoon vanilla extract

Instructions:
1. In a saucepan, combine the water, sugar, salt, and vegetable oil. Bring the mixture to a boil over medium heat.

2. Remove the saucepan from the heat and add the flour all at once.

Stir vigorously with a wooden spoon until the mixture forms a smooth and sticky dough.

3. Transfer the churro dough to a piping bag fitted with a large star-shaped tip.

4. In a large skillet or deep-fryer, heat vegetable oil to a temperature of 375°F (190°C).

5. Carefully pipe the churro dough into the hot oil, using a knife or scissors to cut off each churro at about 4-6 inches in length.

 Fry the churros in batches, turning them occasionally, until they become golden brown and crispy.

This process usually takes around 4-6 minutes.

Use a slotted spoon or tongs to remove the churros from the oil and transfer them to a paper towel-lined plate to drain excess oil.

6. In a small saucepan, heat the milk over medium heat until it starts to simmer.

7. Add the chopped dark chocolate, sugar, and vanilla extract to the simmering milk.

Whisk the mixture continuously until the chocolate is completely melted and the sauce is smooth and velvety. Remove the saucepan from the heat.

8. Serve the churros warm, either on a plate or in a paper cone.

Dust them with powdered sugar if desired.

9. Serve the warm chocolate dipping sauce alongside the churros.

10. Dip the crispy churros into the rich and creamy chocolate sauce, savoring the delightful combination of textures and flavors.

11. Churros con Chocolate is a beloved Spanish treat enjoyed as a snack or dessert.

Enjoy the crispy fried dough with its soft interior, generously coated in sugar, and the luscious chocolate sauce that adds a touch of indulgence.

Que aproveche!

ii. Recipe: Crema Catalana

Ingredients:
- 4 cups whole milk
- 1 cinnamon stick
- 1 lemon peel (strips)
- 1 vanilla bean, split lengthwise
- 6 large egg yolks
- 3/4 cup granulated sugar
- 3 tablespoons cornstarch
- Granulated sugar (for caramelizing the top)
- Fresh berries or mint leaves (for garnish)

Instructions:
1. In a medium saucepan, pour the milk and add the cinnamon stick, lemon peel, and vanilla bean. Heat the mixture over medium heat until it starts to simmer.

Once simmering, remove the pan from the heat and set it aside to infuse for about 15 minutes.

2. In a mixing bowl, whisk together the egg yolks, granulated sugar, and cornstarch until well combined and smooth.

3. Remove the cinnamon stick, lemon peel, and vanilla bean from the milk mixture.

Gradually pour the warm milk into the egg yolk mixture while whisking continuously.

4. Return the mixture to the saucepan and cook it over medium heat, stirring constantly with a wooden spoon or whisk.

Continue cooking until the mixture thickens and coats the back of the spoon.

This usually takes about 10-15 minutes. Be careful not to let it boil.

5. Once the crema catalana has thickened, remove the saucepan from the heat.

Pour the mixture into individual ramekins or shallow dishes, dividing it evenly.

6. Allow the crema catalana to cool at room temperature for a few minutes, then refrigerate it for at least 2 hours or until chilled and set.

7. Just before serving, sprinkle a thin, even layer of granulated sugar on top of each crema catalana.

8. To caramelize the sugar, you can use a kitchen blowtorch or place the ramekins under a broiler set to high heat.

Watch carefully, as the sugar can quickly burn.

Once caramelized, allow the sugar to harden for a few minutes.

9. Garnish the crema catalana with fresh berries or mint leaves for an extra touch of freshness and presentation.

10. Serve the chilled and caramelized Crema Catalana as a delightful dessert.

Break through the crisp caramelized sugar to reveal the creamy and smooth custard underneath.

Enjoy the subtle flavors of cinnamon, lemon, and vanilla in this classic Catalan dessert.

 Buen provecho!

3.14. Greek Mezze and Souvlaki:

Greek cuisine offers a harmonious blend of Mediterranean flavors and fresh ingredients.

Embrace the concept of Mezze, an array of small dishes perfect for sharing.

Create a mezze platter with Tzatziki, Hummus, Dolmades, and Spanakopita.

Recipe: Mezze Platter

Ingredients:
- Hummus

- Tzatziki
- Baba ganoush
- Tabouli
- Falafel
- Pita bread or pita chips
- Olives (assorted varieties)
- Feta cheese, cubed or crumbled
- Cherry tomatoes
- Cucumber, sliced
- Fresh mint leaves (for garnish)
- Lemon wedges (for serving)

Instructions:
1. Prepare the hummus, tzatziki, baba ganoush, tabouli, and falafel according to their respective recipes.

You can find individual recipes for each of these mezze items in this cookbook.

2. Once the mezze items are ready, arrange them on a large platter or serving tray.

3. Place a bowl of hummus in the center of the platter.

Surround it with dollops of tzatziki and baba ganoush, evenly spaced apart.

4. Spread the tabouli salad in a pile next to the hummus bowl.

5. Arrange the falafel in a separate section of the platter, either in a row or a cluster.

6. Fill in the remaining space on the platter with pita bread or pita chips, olives, feta cheese, cherry tomatoes, and cucumber slices.

7. Garnish the mezze platter with fresh mint leaves for a pop of color and freshness.

8. Serve the mezze platter with lemon wedges on the side for squeezing over the falafel, hummus, or other items as desired.

9. To enjoy, invite your guests to sample and assemble their own mezze bites.

They can scoop hummus, tzatziki, or baba ganoush onto pita bread, top it with tabouli, falafel, olives, feta cheese, cherry tomatoes, and cucumber slices.

10. The mezze platter offers a delightful variety of flavors and textures, allowing everyone to create their own combinations.

It's a perfect appetizer or snack for gatherings and showcases the rich and vibrant cuisine of the Mediterranean.

Enjoy the colorful and delicious array of mezze!

Buen provecho!

Dive into the world of grilled meats with Souvlaki, marinated skewers of succulent lamb or chicken.

Recipe: Souvlaki

Ingredients:
- 1.5 pounds boneless, skinless chicken breasts or pork tenderloin, cut into 1-inch cubes
- 1/4 cup olive oil
- 3 tablespoons lemon juice
- 3 cloves garlic, minced
- 1 tablespoon dried oregano
- 1 teaspoon dried thyme

- 1 teaspoon paprika
- Salt and pepper, to taste
- Wooden skewers, soaked in water for 30 minutes

Instructions:
1. In a bowl, combine the olive oil, lemon juice, minced garlic, dried oregano, dried thyme, paprika, salt, and pepper.

Stir well to create the marinade for the souvlaki.

2. Place the chicken or pork cubes in a shallow dish or a resealable plastic bag.

Pour the marinade over the meat, ensuring all the pieces are coated. Marinate in the refrigerator for at least 2 hours, or overnight for best results.

Turn the meat occasionally to ensure even marination.

3. Preheat your grill or grill pan to medium-high heat.

4. Thread the marinated meat onto the soaked wooden skewers, dividing them evenly.

5. Place the skewers on the preheated grill or grill pan and cook for about 10-12 minutes, turning occasionally, until the meat is cooked through and slightly charred on the edges.

6. Remove the skewers from the grill and let them rest for a few minutes before serving.

7. Serve the souvlaki hot, either on or off the skewers.

You can accompany it with traditional Greek sides like pita bread, tzatziki sauce, sliced tomatoes, onions, and cucumber.

8. Enjoy the succulent and flavorful Greek Souvlaki, where tender pieces of marinated chicken or pork are grilled to perfection.

The combination of citrusy marinade and aromatic herbs infuses the meat with a mouthwatering taste. It's a delicious and satisfying dish that brings a taste of Greece to your table.

Kali orexi!

Experience the comfort of Greek Moussaka and savor the simplicity of a Greek Salad.

Let the flavors of olive oil, lemon, and feta cheese transport you to the shores of Greece.

i. Recipe: Greek Moussaka

Ingredients:
For the meat sauce:
- 1.5 pounds ground lamb or beef
- 1 large onion, finely chopped
- 3 cloves garlic, minced
- 1 can (14 ounces) diced tomatoes
- 2 tablespoons tomato paste
- 1 teaspoon dried oregano
- 1/2 teaspoon ground cinnamon
- Salt and pepper, to taste
- Olive oil, for cooking

For the eggplant layers:
- 2 large eggplants, sliced lengthwise into 1/4-inch thick slices
- Salt, for sprinkling
- Olive oil, for brushing

For the béchamel sauce:
- 4 tablespoons butter
- 1/4 cup all-purpose flour
- 2 cups milk
- 1/4 teaspoon ground nutmeg
- Salt and pepper, to taste
- 2 large eggs, beaten

Instructions:
1. Preheat your oven to 375°F (190°C).

2. Prepare the meat sauce: In a large skillet, heat olive oil over medium heat.

Add the chopped onion and minced garlic, and sauté until they become translucent and fragrant.

 Add the ground lamb or beef and cook until browned. Drain any excess fat from the skillet.

3. Stir in the diced tomatoes, tomato paste, dried oregano, ground cinnamon, salt, and pepper.

 Simmer the sauce for about 15-20 minutes, allowing the flavors to meld together.

Remove the skillet from the heat and set it aside.

4. Prepare the eggplant layers:
Place the eggplant slices on a baking sheet or a cutting board.

Sprinkle them with salt and let them sit for about 20 minutes to draw out excess moisture.

Rinse the eggplant slices under cold water and pat them dry with paper towels.

5. Brush the eggplant slices lightly with olive oil on both sides.

Heat a grill pan or skillet over medium heat and cook the eggplant slices in batches until they become tender and slightly charred.

Set the cooked eggplant slices aside.

6. Prepare the béchamel sauce: In a saucepan, melt the butter over medium heat.

Stir in the flour and cook for about 2 minutes, stirring constantly, to make a roux.

Gradually whisk in the milk, nutmeg, salt, and pepper.

Cook the sauce, stirring constantly, until it thickens and coats the back of a spoon.

Remove the saucepan from the heat.

7. Beat the eggs in a separate bowl. Gradually whisk a small amount of the hot béchamel sauce into the beaten eggs, tempering them.

Then, pour the egg mixture back into the saucepan with the remaining béchamel sauce, whisking constantly.

8. Assemble the moussaka: In a greased baking dish, spread a layer of cooked eggplant slices on the bottom.

Top the eggplant with a layer of the meat sauce.

Repeat the layers, ending with a layer of meat sauce on top.

9. Pour the béchamel sauce evenly over the top layer of meat sauce, spreading it with a spatula to cover the entire surface.

10. Place the moussaka in the preheated oven and bake for about 45-50 minutes, or until the top turns golden brown and bubbly.

11. Remove the moussaka from the oven and let it rest for 15-20 minutes before serving.

This allows the layers to set and the flavors to meld together.

12. Slice the moussaka into squares or rectangles, and serve it warm as a main course.

It pairs well with a Greek salad and crusty bread.

13. Enjoy the rich and comforting Greek Moussaka, a layered casserole of eggplant, meat sauce, and creamy béchamel sauce.

The combination of flavors and textures creates a hearty and satisfying dish that is a staple in Greek cuisine.

It's perfect for sharing with family and friends.

Note: Moussaka can also be prepared ahead of time and refrigerated.

Simply reheat it in the oven before serving.

Enjoy this classic Greek dish, savoring each bite of tender eggplant, flavorful meat sauce, and creamy béchamel. It's a taste of

Greece that will transport you to the Mediterranean with its rich and comforting flavors.

Kali orexi!

ii. Recipe: Greek Salad

Ingredients:
- 4 cups romaine lettuce, torn into bite-sized pieces
- 1 large cucumber, diced
- 2 large tomatoes, diced
- 1/2 red onion, thinly sliced
- 1/2 cup Kalamata olives, pitted
- 1/2 cup crumbled feta cheese
- 1/4 cup extra virgin olive oil
- 2 tablespoons red wine vinegar
- 1 teaspoon dried oregano
- Salt and pepper, to taste

Instructions:
1. In a large salad bowl, combine the torn romaine lettuce, diced cucumber, diced tomatoes, thinly sliced red onion, and Kalamata olives.

2. In a small bowl, whisk together the extra virgin olive oil, red wine vinegar, dried oregano, salt, and pepper. This will be the dressing for the Greek salad.

3. Drizzle the dressing over the salad ingredients in the bowl. Toss gently to coat all the ingredients with the dressing.

4. Sprinkle the crumbled feta cheese over the top of the salad.

5. Serve the Greek salad immediately as a refreshing and vibrant side dish or light meal.

6. Enjoy the medley of flavors in the Greek salad, from the crisp lettuce and cucumber to the juicy tomatoes and tangy feta cheese.

The combination of ingredients and the classic dressing capture the essence of Greek cuisine.

It's a perfect accompaniment to grilled meats, fish, or as a standalone dish.

Kali orexi!

3.15. British Pub Fare:

British pub fare is all about hearty comfort food that warms the soul. Embrace the classics like Fish and Chips, Bangers and Mash, or Shepherd's Pie.

i. Recipe: Fish and Chips

Ingredients:
For the fish:
- 1 pound white fish fillets (such as cod or haddock)
- 1 cup all-purpose flour
- 1 teaspoon baking powder
- 1/2 teaspoon salt
- 1/2 teaspoon paprika
- 1 cup cold sparkling water
- Vegetable oil, for frying

For the chips:
- 4 large russet potatoes
- Vegetable oil, for frying
- Salt, to taste

Instructions:
1. Preheat your oven to 200°C (400°F).

2. Prepare the fish: In a shallow bowl, whisk together the flour, baking powder, salt, and paprika.

Slowly pour in the sparkling water while whisking, until a smooth batter forms.

Let the batter rest for about 10 minutes.

3. Cut the fish fillets into thick strips. Pat them dry with paper towels.

4. In a deep frying pan or Dutch oven, heat vegetable oil to a depth of about 2 inches over medium-high heat.

5. Dip the fish strips into the batter, allowing any excess batter to drip off.

Carefully place the coated fish into the hot oil, a few pieces at a time.

Fry until golden brown and crispy, about 3-4 minutes per side.

Transfer the cooked fish to a baking sheet lined with paper towels to drain excess oil.

Keep the cooked fish warm in the preheated oven while frying the remaining batches.

6. Prepare the chips: Peel the potatoes and cut them into thick, even-sized chips or fries.

7. Rinse the cut potatoes under cold water to remove excess starch.

Pat them dry with paper towels.

8. In the same frying pan or Dutch oven, heat vegetable oil to a depth of about 2 inches over medium-high heat.

9. Carefully add the potato chips to the hot oil, a few at a time, and fry until golden brown and crispy, about 5-7 minutes.

Use a slotted spoon or a spider strainer to remove the chips from the oil.

Transfer them to a paper towel-lined baking sheet to drain excess oil.

10. Season the freshly fried chips with salt while they are still hot.

11. Serve the crispy fish and chips together on a platter.

Accompany them with tartar sauce, malt vinegar, or ketchup, as desired.

12. Enjoy the classic British dish of Fish and Chips, with its crispy battered fish and golden fries.

It's a delicious and comforting meal that brings a taste of the UK to your table.

Perfect for a casual dinner or a fun gathering.

Enjoy!

Note: For a healthier version, you can bake the fish and oven-roast the chips instead of frying them.

Simply coat the fish with a light brushing of oil and bake at 200°C (400°F) for about 15-20 minutes until cooked through and golden.

Toss the potato chips with a little oil, spread them on a baking sheet, and bake at 200°C (400°F) for about 30-35 minutes, flipping them halfway through, until crispy and golden brown.

ii. Recipe: Bangers and Mash

Ingredients:
- 8 pork sausages (bangers)
- 4 large potatoes, peeled and cut into chunks
- 1/4 cup milk
- 2 tablespoons unsalted butter
- Salt and pepper, to taste
- 1 onion, thinly sliced
- Gravy (optional)

Instructions:
1. Cook the sausages: Heat a large frying pan over medium heat.

Add the sausages and cook them, turning occasionally, until they are browned and cooked through.

This usually takes about 12-15 minutes. Remove the sausages from the pan and set them aside.

2. Prepare the mashed potatoes: Place the potato chunks in a large pot and cover them with cold water. Add a pinch of salt to the water.

Bring the water to a boil and cook the potatoes until they are fork-tender, about 15-20 minutes.

3. Drain the potatoes and return them to the pot. Add the milk and butter to the pot.

Using a potato masher or a fork, mash the potatoes until they are smooth and creamy. Season with salt and pepper to taste.

4. Cook the onions: In the same frying pan used to cook the sausages, add the thinly sliced onions.

Cook them over medium heat, stirring occasionally, until they are caramelized and golden brown.

This usually takes about 10-15 minutes.

5. Serve: Arrange a generous portion of mashed potatoes on a plate.

Place two cooked sausages on top of the mashed potatoes.

Add a spoonful of caramelized onions on the side. If desired, pour gravy over the sausages and mashed potatoes.

6. Enjoy the classic British dish of Bangers and Mash, where juicy sausages, creamy mashed potatoes, and caramelized onions come together for a hearty and comforting meal.

 It's a beloved favorite that brings warmth and flavor to your table. Perfect for a cozy dinner or a gathering with friends and family.

Enjoy!

iii. Recipe: Shepherd's Pie

Ingredients:
For the mashed potatoes:
- 4 large potatoes, peeled and cut into chunks
- 1/4 cup milk
- 2 tablespoons unsalted butter
- Salt and pepper, to taste

For the filling:
- 1 tablespoon vegetable oil
- 1 onion, diced
- 2 carrots, diced
- 2 cloves garlic, minced

- 1 pound ground lamb or beef
- 2 tablespoons all-purpose flour
- 1 cup beef or vegetable broth
- 1 tablespoon tomato paste
- 1 teaspoon Worcestershire sauce
- 1 teaspoon dried thyme
- 1 cup frozen peas
- Salt and pepper, to taste

Instructions:
1. Preheat your oven to 200°C (400°F).

2. Prepare the mashed potatoes: Place the potato chunks in a large pot and cover them with cold water.

Add a pinch of salt to the water.

 Bring the water to a boil and cook the potatoes until they are fork-tender, about 15-20 minutes.

3. Drain the potatoes and return them to the pot.

Add the milk and butter to the pot.

Using a potato masher or a fork, mash the potatoes until they are smooth and creamy.

Season with salt and pepper to taste. Set aside.

4. Prepare the filling: In a large skillet, heat the vegetable oil over medium heat.

Add the diced onion and carrots and cook until they begin to soften, about 5 minutes.

Add the minced garlic and cook for an additional minute.

5. Add the ground lamb or beef to the skillet and cook, breaking it up with a spoon, until browned and cooked through.

Sprinkle the flour over the meat and vegetables, stirring to coat evenly.

6. Pour in the beef or vegetable broth, tomato paste, Worcestershire sauce, and dried thyme.

Stir well to combine. Bring the mixture to a simmer and let it cook for about 5 minutes, until the sauce thickens slightly.

7. Stir in the frozen peas and cook for another 2-3 minutes.

Season with salt and pepper to taste.

8. Assemble the Shepherd's Pie: Transfer the meat and vegetable filling to a baking dish or individual ramekins.

Spread the mashed potatoes evenly over the top, covering the filling completely.

9. Use a fork to create some texture on the surface of the mashed potatoes.

This will help them brown nicely in the oven.

10. Place the baking dish or ramekins on a baking sheet and place it in the preheated oven.

Bake for 25-30 minutes, or until the top is golden brown and the filling is bubbly.

11. Remove from the oven and let it cool for a few minutes before serving.

12. Serve the Shepherd's Pie hot, enjoying the comforting layers of flavorful meat and vegetables topped with creamy mashed potatoes.

It's a classic dish that is perfect for a satisfying family meal or a gathering with loved ones.

Enjoy the deliciousness of this hearty comfort food!

Discover the joy of making your own fluffy Yorkshire puddings and delectable Sticky Toffee Pudding.

i. Recipe: Yorkshire Puddings

Ingredients:
- 1 cup all-purpose flour
- 1/2 teaspoon salt
- 1 cup milk
- 2 large eggs
- Vegetable oil, for greasing the muffin tin

Instructions:
1. Preheat your oven to 220°C (425°F).

2. In a mixing bowl, whisk together the flour and salt.

3. In a separate bowl, whisk together the milk and eggs until well combined.

4. Gradually pour the milk and egg mixture into the bowl with the flour mixture.

Whisk until you have a smooth batter with no lumps.

5. Let the batter rest for about 30 minutes at room temperature.

This allows the gluten to relax and helps achieve a lighter texture.

6. While the batter is resting, grease a muffin tin with vegetable oil.

Make sure to grease the bottom and sides of each cup.

7. Place the greased muffin tin in the preheated oven for about 5 minutes, or until the oil is hot and sizzling.

8. Carefully remove the hot muffin tin from the oven and quickly pour the batter into the cups, filling each one about halfway.

9. Return the muffin tin to the oven and bake for 20-25 minutes, or until the Yorkshire puddings are puffed up and golden brown.

10. Avoid opening the oven door during baking, as this can cause the puddings to deflate.

11. Once baked, remove the Yorkshire puddings from the oven and transfer them to a wire rack to cool slightly.

12. Serve the Yorkshire puddings immediately while they are still hot and crispy.

They are traditionally enjoyed as a side dish with roast beef and gravy.

However, they can also be served with other meats or used as a base for savory fillings like sausages or vegetables.

13. Enjoy these light and airy golden puffs of goodness as a delightful accompaniment to your favorite roast dinner or as a delicious snack.

Yorkshire puddings are a classic British treat that adds a touch of elegance to any meal.

ii. Recipe: Sticky Toffee Pudding

Ingredients:
For the pudding:
- 1 cup pitted dates, chopped
- 1 cup boiling water
- 1 teaspoon baking soda
- 1 cup all-purpose flour
- 1 teaspoon baking powder
- 1/2 teaspoon salt
- 1/2 cup unsalted butter, softened
- 3/4 cup granulated sugar
- 2 large eggs
- 1 teaspoon vanilla extract

For the toffee sauce:
- 1 cup heavy cream
- 1 cup packed brown sugar
- 1/2 cup unsalted butter
- 1 teaspoon vanilla extract

Instructions:
1. Preheat your oven to 180°C (350°F).

Grease a baking dish or individual ramekins with butter.

2. In a bowl, place the chopped dates and pour the boiling water over them.

Stir in the baking soda and let the mixture sit for about 15 minutes to soften the dates.

3. In a separate bowl, whisk together the flour, baking powder, and salt.

4. In a large mixing bowl, cream together the softened butter and granulated sugar until light and fluffy.

5. Add the eggs, one at a time, beating well after each addition. Stir in the vanilla extract.

6. Gradually add the dry flour mixture to the butter-sugar mixture, alternating with the date mixture.

Begin and end with the dry ingredients, mixing until just combined.

7. Pour the batter into the greased baking dish or ramekins, spreading it evenly.

8. Bake in the preheated oven for 25-30 minutes, or until a toothpick inserted into the center comes out clean.

9. While the pudding is baking, prepare the toffee sauce.

In a saucepan, combine the heavy cream, brown sugar, butter, and vanilla extract.

 Heat over medium heat, stirring constantly, until the sugar has dissolved and the sauce is smooth and thickened.

Remove from heat.

10. Once the pudding is baked, remove it from the oven and let it cool for a few minutes.

11. To serve, cut the warm pudding into slices or scoop it into individual bowls.

Drizzle the warm toffee sauce generously over each portion.

12. You can also serve the pudding with a scoop of vanilla ice cream or a dollop of whipped cream for added indulgence.

13. Enjoy the rich and decadent Sticky Toffee Pudding, with its moist date-filled cake and luscious toffee sauce.

It's a classic British dessert that will satisfy any and leave you craving more.

Perfect for special occasions or as a comforting treat on a cozy evening.

Embrace the flavors of Europe as you embark on this culinary journey.

From the elegance of French cuisine to the rustic charm of British pub fare, each cuisine offers its own distinct character and flavors.

Explore the traditions, techniques, and ingredients that have made European cuisines beloved across the globe.

Get to savor the diverse delights of Europe and let your taste buds be your guide.

Bon appétit! Buon appetito! Buen provecho! Καλή όρεξη! Enjoy your meal!

Chapter 4: Asian Sensations

Section 1: Chinese Dim Sum and Stir-Fries

- Introduction to Chinese Cuisine

Chinese cuisine is renowned for its rich flavors, diverse ingredients, and intricate cooking techniques.

With a culinary history spanning thousands of years, Chinese cuisine offers a vast array of regional specialties that showcase the country's unique culinary heritage.

1. Regional Diversity:
China is a vast country with diverse regional cuisines, each with its own distinct flavors and ingredients.

From the fiery flavors of Sichuan cuisine to the delicate and refined dishes of Cantonese cuisine, Chinese cuisine embodies a rich tapestry of flavors and techniques.

2. Key Ingredients:
Chinese cooking relies on a wide range of ingredients that contribute to its distinctive flavors.

Some of the essential ingredients used in Chinese cuisine include soy sauce, ginger, garlic, scallions, sesame oil, and a variety of aromatic spices.

These ingredients are combined in various ways to create complex and balanced flavors.

3. Cooking Techniques:
Chinese cooking employs a variety of cooking techniques that contribute to the unique taste and texture of the dishes.

Stir-frying, steaming, braising, deep-frying, and quick blanching are some of the commonly used techniques.

Each method is carefully chosen to enhance the flavors and retain the natural textures of the ingredients.

4. Dim Sum Tradition:
Dim sum, meaning "touch the heart" in Cantonese, is a traditional Chinese dining experience that consists of bite-sized portions of food served in small steamer baskets or on small plates.

Dim sum includes a wide range of dishes such as dumplings, steamed buns, rice rolls, and various savory snacks.

It is often enjoyed during brunch or as a communal meal with family and friends.

5. Stir-Fried Delights:
Stir-frying is a popular cooking method in Chinese cuisine that involves quickly cooking ingredients over high heat in a wok.

This technique allows for the preservation of nutrients, vibrant colors, and distinct flavors of the ingredients.

Stir-fried dishes often combine a variety of vegetables, meats, and sauces, resulting in delicious and balanced meals.

As you embark on your culinary journey through Chinese cuisine, get ready to savor the harmonious blend of flavors, vibrant colors, and enticing aromas that make it truly remarkable.

Whether you're exploring the intricate world of dim sum or indulging in the sizzling delights of stir-fries, Chinese cuisine is sure to captivate your taste buds and leave you craving for more.

- Dim Sum Delights

Dim sum is a beloved culinary tradition in Chinese cuisine, offering a delightful assortment of bite-sized dishes that are perfect for sharing and enjoying with friends and family.

These small, steamed or fried delicacies are bursting with flavors and textures, showcasing the culinary expertise and creativity of Chinese chefs.

i. Steamed Shrimp Dumplings (Har Gow) Recipe:

Ingredients:
- 250g fresh shrimp, peeled and deveined
- 1 tablespoon cornstarch
- 1 tablespoon soy sauce
- 1 teaspoon sesame oil
- 1 teaspoon sugar
- 1/4 teaspoon white pepper
- 1/4 teaspoon salt
- 1/2 cup water chestnuts, finely chopped
- 1/4 cup green onions, finely chopped
- 20 round dumpling wrappers

Instructions:
1. In a mixing bowl, combine the shrimp, cornstarch, soy sauce, sesame oil, sugar, white pepper, and salt. Mix well to coat the shrimp evenly.

2. Add the water chestnuts and green onions to the shrimp mixture. Stir until all the ingredients are well combined.

3. Take one dumpling wrapper and place a tablespoon of the shrimp mixture in the center.

Wet the edges of the wrapper with water and fold it in half, pressing the edges together to seal.

Pleat the edges of the dumpling for an attractive appearance, if desired.

4. Repeat the process with the remaining dumpling wrappers and shrimp mixture.

5. Place the dumplings on a steamer lined with parchment paper or cabbage leaves, leaving some space between each dumpling.

6. Steam the dumplings over high heat for about 8-10 minutes or until the shrimp is cooked through and the dumpling wrappers become translucent.

7. Carefully remove the steamed shrimp dumplings from the steamer and serve hot with soy sauce, chili oil, or your favorite dipping sauce.

Enjoy the delicate and savory Steamed Shrimp Dumplings (Har Gow) as a delightful appetizer or as part of a dim sum feast.

The combination of succulent shrimp, crunchy water chestnuts, and aromatic seasonings wrapped in a tender dumpling wrapper is sure to please your taste buds and transport you to the vibrant world of dim sum.

ii. Pork Siu Mai Recipe:

Ingredients:
- 250g ground pork

- 1/4 cup shrimp, finely chopped
- 2 tablespoons water chestnuts, finely chopped
- 1 tablespoon soy sauce
- 1 tablespoon oyster sauce
- 1 teaspoon sesame oil
- 1 teaspoon cornstarch
- 1/2 teaspoon sugar
- 1/4 teaspoon white pepper
- 1/4 teaspoon salt
- 20 round dumpling wrappers
- Green peas or carrot slices, for garnish

Instructions:
1. In a mixing bowl, combine the ground pork, chopped shrimp, water chestnuts, soy sauce, oyster sauce, sesame oil, cornstarch, sugar, white pepper, and salt.

Mix well until all the ingredients are thoroughly combined.

2. Take one dumpling wrapper and place a tablespoon of the pork mixture in the center.

Wet the edges of the wrapper with water and gently pinch the edges together, creating pleats around the filling.

Leave the top open and expose some of the filling.

Place a green pea or carrot slice on top for garnish, if desired.

3. Repeat the process with the remaining dumpling wrappers and pork mixture.

4. Place the siu mai on a steamer lined with parchment paper or cabbage leaves, leaving some space between each dumpling.

5. Steam the siu mai over high heat for about 12-15 minutes or until the pork is cooked through and the dumpling wrappers become slightly translucent.

6. Carefully remove the steamed pork siu mai from the steamer and serve hot with soy sauce or your favorite dipping sauce.

Indulge in the succulent and flavorful Pork Siu Mai, a classic dim sum delicacy that is sure to impress your taste buds.

 The combination of tender ground pork, chopped shrimp, and aromatic seasonings wrapped in a delicate dumpling wrapper creates a perfect balance of textures and flavors.

Enjoy these delightful morsels as a tasty appetizer or as part of a dim sum feast.

iii. BBQ Pork Buns (Char Siu Bao) Recipe:

Ingredients:
- 250g char siu (barbecue pork), diced
- 2 tablespoons hoisin sauce
- 1 tablespoon soy sauce
- 1 tablespoon oyster sauce
- 1 tablespoon sugar
- 1 teaspoon sesame oil
- 1/4 teaspoon five-spice powder
- 1 cup all-purpose flour
- 1/2 cup warm water
- 1 tablespoon vegetable oil
- 1 teaspoon baking powder
- 1/4 teaspoon salt

Instructions:

1. In a mixing bowl, combine the diced char siu, hoisin sauce, soy sauce, oyster sauce, sugar, sesame oil, and five-spice powder.

Mix well until the char siu is coated with the sauce. Set aside.

2. In a separate bowl, prepare the dough by combining the all-purpose flour, warm water, vegetable oil, baking powder, and salt.

Mix until a soft and elastic dough forms. Knead the dough for a few minutes until it becomes smooth.

3. Cover the dough with a clean cloth and let it rest for about 20 minutes to allow it to rise.

4. After the resting period, divide the dough into small equal-sized portions and roll each portion into a small circle about 4 inches in diameter.

5. Place a spoonful of the char siu filling in the center of each dough circle. Gather the edges of the dough and pinch them together, sealing the filling inside.

6. Place the filled buns on small squares of parchment paper and arrange them on a steamer tray.

7. Steam the BBQ pork buns over high heat for about 15-20 minutes or until the dough is fluffy and cooked through.

8. Carefully remove the steamed BBQ pork buns from the steamer and serve them warm.

Enjoy the mouthwatering BBQ Pork Buns (Char Siu Bao), a classic dim sum favorite.

The soft and fluffy steamed buns filled with savory and sweet char siu create a delightful combination of flavors.

These buns are perfect as a snack, appetizer, or even as a meal on their own.

Savor the taste of this iconic dim sum dish and transport yourself to the bustling streets of Hong Kong.

iv. Egg Custard Tarts Recipe:

Ingredients:
- 1 package ready-made puff pastry
- 3/4 cup granulated sugar
- 1/4 cup water
- 3/4 cup whole milk
- 3/4 cup heavy cream
- 4 large eggs
- 1 teaspoon vanilla extract
- Ground nutmeg, for sprinkling (optional)

Instructions:
1. Preheat your oven to 375°F (190°C) and lightly grease a muffin tin.

2. Roll out the puff pastry on a floured surface until it is about 1/8 inch thick.

Use a round cutter slightly larger than the size of your muffin tin holes to cut out circles of pastry.

Gently press each pastry circle into the muffin tin holes, forming a tart shell.

Set aside.

3. In a saucepan, combine the granulated sugar and water over medium heat.

Stir until the sugar has dissolved, and the mixture comes to a simmer.

Remove from heat and let it cool slightly.

4. In a separate bowl, whisk together the whole milk, heavy cream, eggs, and vanilla extract until well combined.

5. Slowly pour the milk mixture into the cooled sugar syrup, whisking continuously until fully incorporated.

6. Carefully pour the custard mixture into the prepared pastry shells, filling them about 2/3 of the way.

7. Optional: Sprinkle a pinch of ground nutmeg on top of each tart for added flavor.

8. Place the muffin tin in the preheated oven and bake for about 20-25 minutes or until the custard is set and the pastry turns golden brown.

9. Once baked, remove the egg custard tarts from the oven and let them cool in the muffin tin for a few minutes.

Then transfer them to a wire rack to cool completely before serving.

Enjoy the delightful Egg Custard Tarts, a popular dim sum treat that combines a crisp and flaky pastry shell with a smooth and creamy custard filling.

These tarts are a perfect balance of sweetness and richness, making them a beloved dessert option.

Serve them warm or at room temperature for a delightful sweet ending to your dim sum feast or as a standalone treat for any occasion.

Flavorful Stir-Fries

Stir-frying is a cooking technique that originated in China and has become a popular method for preparing quick and delicious meals around the world.

It involves quickly cooking bite-sized pieces of meat, vegetables, and sauces in a hot wok or skillet, resulting in dishes bursting with flavor and vibrant colors.

Here are a few recipes for flavorful stir-fries that will transport your taste buds to the heart of Asian cuisine.

i. Beef and Broccoli Stir-Fry Recipe:

Ingredients:
- 1 lb (450g) beef sirloin, thinly sliced
- 2 cups broccoli florets
- 1 red bell pepper, thinly sliced
- 3 cloves garlic, minced
- 2 tablespoons soy sauce
- 1 tablespoon oyster sauce
- 1 tablespoon hoisin sauce
- 1 tablespoon cornstarch
- 1 teaspoon sesame oil
- 2 tablespoons vegetable oil
- Salt and pepper, to taste

Instructions:

1. In a small bowl, whisk together the soy sauce, oyster sauce, hoisin sauce, cornstarch, and sesame oil. Set aside.

2. Heat the vegetable oil in a wok or large skillet over high heat.

Add the beef slices and stir-fry for 2-3 minutes or until browned.

Remove the beef from the wok and set aside.

3. In the same wok, add the minced garlic and stir-fry for about 30 seconds until fragrant.

4. Add the broccoli florets and red bell pepper to the wok and stir-fry for 3-4 minutes until the vegetables are tender-crisp.

5. Return the cooked beef to the wok and pour in the sauce mixture.

Stir-fry for an additional 1-2 minutes until the sauce thickens and coats the beef and vegetables.

6. Season with salt and pepper to taste.

7. Serve the beef and broccoli stir-fry hot over steamed rice or noodles.

Enjoy the tender beef slices, crisp broccoli, and vibrant flavors of the savory sauce in this classic Beef and Broccoli Stir-Fry.

The combination of the tender meat, crisp vegetables, and umami-rich sauce creates a perfect harmony of textures and tastes.

This dish is not only quick and easy to prepare but also a satisfying and nutritious option for any mealtime.

ii. Kung Pao Chicken Recipe:

Ingredients:
- 1 lb (450g) boneless, skinless chicken breast, cut into bite-sized pieces
- 1/2 cup unsalted peanuts
- 1 red bell pepper, diced
- 1 green bell pepper, diced
- 1/2 cup diced onions
- 3 cloves garlic, minced
- 2 tablespoons soy sauce
- 1 tablespoon hoisin sauce
- 1 tablespoon rice vinegar
- 1 tablespoon cornstarch
- 1 teaspoon sugar
- 1/2 teaspoon red pepper flakes (adjust to taste)
- 2 tablespoons vegetable oil
- Sliced green onions, for garnish

Instructions:
1. In a small bowl, whisk together the soy sauce, hoisin sauce, rice vinegar, cornstarch, sugar, and red pepper flakes. Set aside.

2. Heat the vegetable oil in a wok or large skillet over high heat.

Add the diced chicken and stir-fry for 5-6 minutes or until cooked through and slightly browned.

Remove the chicken from the wok and set aside.

3. In the same wok, add the minced garlic, diced onions, and bell peppers. Stir-fry for about 2-3 minutes until the vegetables are crisp-tender.

4. Return the cooked chicken to the wok and pour in the sauce mixture.

Stir-fry for an additional 2-3 minutes until the sauce thickens and coats the chicken and vegetables.

5. Add the peanuts to the wok and stir to combine.

6. Remove from heat and garnish with sliced green onions.

7. Serve the Kung Pao Chicken hot over steamed rice.

Savor the bold and spicy flavors of Kung Pao Chicken, a classic Chinese stir-fry dish that combines tender chicken, crunchy peanuts, and vibrant vegetables in a savory and tangy sauce.

The dish is known for its distinct combination of heat, sweetness, and umami.

 Enjoy the perfect balance of textures and flavors that will take your taste buds on a delicious adventure.

iii. Sweet and Sour Pork Recipe:

Ingredients:
- 1 lb (450g) pork tenderloin, cut into bite-sized pieces
- 1/2 cup pineapple chunks (fresh or canned)
- 1 red bell pepper, diced
- 1 green bell pepper, diced
- 1/2 cup diced onions
- 3 cloves garlic, minced
- 1/4 cup ketchup
- 2 tablespoons rice vinegar
- 2 tablespoons soy sauce
- 2 tablespoons brown sugar
- 1 tablespoon cornstarch
- 1/2 teaspoon ginger powder
- Vegetable oil, for frying

- Salt and pepper, to taste
- Sliced green onions, for garnish

Instructions:
1. In a small bowl, whisk together the ketchup, rice vinegar, soy sauce, brown sugar, cornstarch, and ginger powder. Set aside.

2. Season the pork pieces with salt and pepper.

3. Heat vegetable oil in a deep skillet or wok over medium-high heat.

Fry the pork pieces until golden brown and cooked through.

Remove the pork from the skillet and set aside on a paper towel-lined plate.

4. In the same skillet, add the minced garlic, diced onions, and bell peppers.

Stir-fry for about 2-3 minutes until the vegetables are crisp-tender.

5. Add the pineapple chunks to the skillet and stir to combine with the vegetables.

6. Pour the sauce mixture into the skillet and bring it to a simmer.

Cook for 1-2 minutes, stirring constantly, until the sauce thickens.

7. Return the cooked pork to the skillet and toss to coat it with the sweet and sour sauce.

8. Remove from heat and garnish with sliced green onions.

9. Serve the Sweet and Sour Pork hot over steamed rice.

Indulge in the delightful flavors of Sweet and Sour Pork, a beloved Chinese dish that combines crispy pork, tangy pineapple, and colorful bell peppers in a sticky and flavorful sauce.

The combination of sweet and sour notes creates a harmonious taste that is both comforting and satisfying.

Enjoy this classic dish that is sure to please your taste buds with its enticing blend of textures and flavors.

Iv. General Tso's Tofu Recipe:

Ingredients:
- 1 block (14 oz) firm tofu, drained and cut into cubes
- 1/4 cup cornstarch
- 2 tablespoons vegetable oil, for frying
- 3 cloves garlic, minced
- 1 tablespoon fresh ginger, grated
- 1/4 cup low-sodium soy sauce
- 2 tablespoons rice vinegar
- 2 tablespoons hoisin sauce
- 2 tablespoons brown sugar
- 1 teaspoon sriracha sauce (adjust to taste)
- 1/4 cup water
- 1 tablespoon cornstarch, dissolved in 2 tablespoons water
- Sliced green onions, for garnish
- Sesame seeds, for garnish

Instructions:
1. Preheat the oven to 400°F (200°C). Line a baking sheet with parchment paper.

2. Place the tofu cubes on the prepared baking sheet. Sprinkle cornstarch over the tofu and toss gently to coat.

3. Bake the tofu in the preheated oven for 20-25 minutes, or until it becomes crispy and golden brown. Remove from the oven and set aside.

4. In a wok or large skillet, heat the vegetable oil over medium-high heat.

Add the minced garlic and grated ginger, and stir-fry for about 1 minute until fragrant.

5. In a small bowl, whisk together the soy sauce, rice vinegar, hoisin sauce, brown sugar, sriracha sauce, and water.

Pour the sauce mixture into the wok and bring it to a simmer.

6. Add the baked tofu cubes to the wok and toss gently to coat them with the sauce.

7. Pour the dissolved cornstarch into the wok and stir well to thicken the sauce.

8. Remove from heat and garnish with sliced green onions and sesame seeds.

9. Serve the General Tso's Tofu hot over steamed rice.

Enjoy the tantalizing flavors of General Tso's Tofu, a vegetarian twist on the popular Chinese dish.

This version features crispy and flavorful tofu cubes coated in a savory and slightly spicy sauce.

The combination of textures and the balance of sweet, tangy, and spicy flavors make this dish a delightful and satisfying choice for both tofu lovers and those seeking a meatless option.

Serve it with steamed rice or noodles for a complete and satisfying meal.

Section 2: Japanese Sushi and Ramen

- Introduction to Japanese Cuisine

Japanese cuisine is renowned for its emphasis on fresh ingredients, elegant presentation, and harmonious flavors.

It is a culinary tradition that values simplicity and balance, allowing the natural flavors of each ingredient to shine.

In this section, we will explore two iconic aspects of Japanese cuisine: Sushi and Ramen.

These beloved dishes have gained popularity worldwide and offer a unique and delicious experience.

Sushi, a dish consisting of vinegared rice topped with various ingredients, showcases the artistry and precision of Japanese cuisine.

From delicate slices of raw fish to vibrant and flavorful vegetable rolls, sushi offers a wide range of options to suit every palate.

The combination of textures, flavors, and beautiful presentation makes sushi a delightful culinary experience.

Ramen, on the other hand, is a comforting and hearty noodle soup that has become a global phenomenon.

This dish features wheat noodles served in a rich and flavorful broth, topped with an array of ingredients such as sliced pork, soft-boiled eggs, nori seaweed, and green onions.

Each region in Japan has its own style of ramen, characterized by different types of broth and toppings, creating a diverse and exciting culinary landscape.

In the upcoming chapters, we will delve into the world of sushi and ramen, exploring their history, techniques, and recipes that will allow you to recreate these Japanese delights in your own kitchen.

Prepare to embark on a culinary journey that celebrates the unique flavors and traditions of Japanese cuisine.

Sushi Delights:

Sushi is not just a dish; it is a culinary art form that combines precision, balance, and creativity.

In this section, we will explore a variety of sushi delights, ranging from classic rolls to innovative creations.

Whether you are a sushi aficionado or new to this Japanese delicacy, there is something for everyone to enjoy.

i. Recipe: Classic Sushi Rolls

Ingredients:
- 2 cups sushi rice
- 4 sheets of nori (seaweed)
- Assorted fillings (e.g., sliced raw fish, cucumber, avocado, crabstick)
- Soy sauce, for dipping

- Wasabi, for serving
- Pickled ginger, for serving

Instructions:
1. Cook the sushi rice according to the package instructions.

Once cooked, let it cool to room temperature.

2. Place a bamboo sushi mat on a flat surface and put a sheet of nori on top of it.

3. Wet your hands with water to prevent the rice from sticking.

Take a handful of sushi rice and evenly spread it on the nori, leaving a small border at the top.

4. Arrange your choice of fillings in a line across the center of the rice.

5. Using the sushi mat, roll the nori and rice tightly around the fillings. Apply gentle pressure to ensure the roll is compact.

6. Wet a sharp knife and slice the sushi roll into bite-sized pieces.

7. Repeat the process with the remaining ingredients.

8. Serve the classic sushi rolls with soy sauce, wasabi, and pickled ginger.

Enjoy the classic sushi rolls, a staple in Japanese cuisine.

These rolls feature a combination of sushi rice and various fillings, creating a harmonious blend of flavors and textures.

Whether you prefer the simplicity of cucumber and avocado or the indulgence of raw fish, each bite offers a delightful experience.

Dip the rolls in soy sauce and add a touch of wasabi for an extra kick of flavor.

Savor the beauty and taste of this iconic sushi creation.

ii. Nigiri Sushi Recipe:

Ingredients:
- Sushi rice (2 cups)
- Fresh fish or seafood (e.g., salmon, tuna, shrimp, eel)
- Soy sauce, for dipping
- Wasabi, for serving
- Pickled ginger, for serving

Instructions:
1. Prepare the sushi rice by cooking it according to the package instructions.

 Once cooked, let it cool to room temperature.

2. Cut the fresh fish or seafood into thin slices.

Ensure that the slices are of a size that can easily fit on top of the sushi rice.

3. Wet your hands with water to prevent the rice from sticking.

Take a small handful of sushi rice and gently shape it into an oblong shape, about 1 inch in length.

4. Place a slice of fish or seafood on top of the shaped sushi rice. Press lightly to ensure it adheres to the rice.

5. Repeat the process with the remaining sushi rice and slices of fish or seafood.

6. Arrange the nigiri sushi on a serving platter.

7. Serve the nigiri sushi with soy sauce, wasabi, and pickled ginger.

Nigiri sushi is a classic and elegant form of sushi that showcases the natural flavors of the fish or seafood.

The simplicity of this dish allows the quality and freshness of the ingredients to shine.

Each piece of nigiri sushi is carefully handcrafted, with the sushi rice acting as a bed for the delicate slices of fish or seafood.

Dip the nigiri sushi into soy sauce, add a touch of wasabi for an extra kick, and cleanse your palate with the pickled ginger.

Indulge in the exquisite flavors and textures of this traditional Japanese delicacy.

Iii. Tempura Rolls Recipe:

Ingredients:
- Sushi rice (2 cups)
- Nori (seaweed) sheets
- Assorted tempura ingredients (e.g., shrimp, vegetables)
- Tempura batter mix
- Vegetable oil, for frying
- Soy sauce, for dipping
- Wasabi, for serving
- Pickled ginger, for serving

Instructions:

1. Cook the sushi rice according to the package instructions. Once cooked, let it cool to room temperature.

2. Prepare the tempura batter mix according to the package instructions.

3. Dip the tempura ingredients (shrimp, vegetables) into the prepared tempura batter, ensuring they are evenly coated.

4. Heat vegetable oil in a deep frying pan or pot to around 350°F (175°C).

5. Fry the tempura ingredients in batches until they turn golden brown and crispy. Remove them from the oil and place them on a paper towel to drain excess oil.

6. Lay a sheet of nori on a bamboo sushi mat.

7. Wet your hands with water to prevent the rice from sticking.

 Take a handful of sushi rice and evenly spread it on the nori, leaving a small border at the top.

8. Arrange the tempura ingredients in a line across the center of the rice.

9. Using the sushi mat, roll the nori and rice tightly around the tempura fillings.

Apply gentle pressure to ensure the roll is compact.

10. Wet a sharp knife and slice the tempura roll into bite-sized pieces.

11. Serve the tempura rolls with soy sauce, wasabi, and pickled ginger.

Tempura rolls offer a delightful twist on traditional sushi, combining the crispiness of tempura-fried ingredients with the softness of sushi rice.

The contrast in textures creates a unique and satisfying eating experience.

Whether you choose to use shrimp, vegetables, or a combination of both, the crispy tempura adds a delightful crunch to each bite.

Dip the tempura rolls in soy sauce, add a touch of wasabi for an extra kick, and cleanse your palate with the pickled ginger.

Enjoy the fusion of flavors and textures in this delectable variation of sushi.

iv. Miso Soup Recipe:

Ingredients:
- Dashi stock (4 cups)
- Miso paste (3-4 tablespoons)
- Tofu, diced (1/2 cup)
- Wakame seaweed, rehydrated and chopped (1/4 cup)
- Green onions, chopped (2 tablespoons)
- Optional: Sliced mushrooms, sliced green beans, or other vegetables of your choice

Instructions:
1. In a pot, bring the dashi stock to a gentle simmer over medium heat.

2. Add the diced tofu and rehydrated wakame seaweed to the pot.

3. If using additional vegetables, add them to the pot and simmer until they are cooked to your desired tenderness.

4. In a small bowl, dilute the miso paste with a little bit of hot broth from the pot. Stir until the miso paste is smooth and dissolved.

5. Gradually add the diluted miso paste back into the pot, stirring gently to incorporate it into the soup.

6. Reduce the heat to low and let the soup simmer for another 2-3 minutes to blend the flavors.

7. Remove the pot from the heat and garnish the soup with chopped green onions.

8. Serve the miso soup hot in individual bowls.

Miso soup is a staple in Japanese cuisine, known for its comforting and umami-rich flavors.

This simple yet satisfying soup is made with a base of dashi stock and miso paste, which provides a unique depth of flavor.

The addition of tofu, wakame seaweed, and optional vegetables creates a hearty and nourishing dish.

Enjoy the warmth and comforting aroma of miso soup, perfect as a starter or a light meal.

(Note: Feel free to customize the miso soup by adding your favorite ingredients.)

Ramen Noodle Bowls:

Ramen, a beloved Japanese dish, has gained worldwide popularity for its flavorful broth and delicious toppings.

In this section, we will explore the art of creating satisfying ramen noodle bowls.

From rich and creamy tonkotsu to refreshing and tangy shoyu, each bowl of ramen offers a unique culinary experience.

Whether you prefer a comforting pork-based broth or a lighter vegetarian option, there's a ramen recipe for every palate.

i. Recipe: Tonkotsu Ramen

Ingredients:
- Pork bones (4-5 pounds)
- Water (8-10 cups)
- Ramen noodles (4 servings)
- Chashu pork (thinly sliced) or pork belly (optional)
- Soft-boiled eggs (1-2 per serving)
- Fresh bean sprouts (1 cup)
- Nori (seaweed) sheets, cut into small pieces
- Green onions, thinly sliced
- Sesame seeds, for garnish
- For the broth:
  - Ginger, sliced (2-inch piece)
  - Garlic cloves, crushed (4-5 cloves)
  - Soy sauce (1/4 cup)
  - Mirin (2 tablespoons)
  - Salt, to taste

Instructions:
1. Start by preparing the broth. In a large pot, add the pork bones and enough water to cover them.

Bring the water to a boil and then lower the heat to a simmer.

2. Skim off any impurities that rise to the surface of the broth.

This step helps ensure a clear and clean-tasting broth.

3. Add the ginger, garlic, soy sauce, mirin, and a pinch of salt to the pot.

Simmer the broth for at least 6-8 hours to extract maximum flavor from the pork bones.

4. Once the broth has simmered, strain it through a fine-mesh sieve, discarding the solids.

This will result in a rich and velvety tonkotsu broth.

5. Cook the ramen noodles according to the package instructions.

Drain and rinse them with cold water to remove excess starch.

6. In a separate pot, bring the tonkotsu broth to a gentle simmer.

7. Arrange the cooked ramen noodles in serving bowls.

Ladle the hot tonkotsu broth over the noodles, ensuring they are fully submerged.

8. Top the bowls with chashu pork slices or pork belly, soft-boiled eggs, bean sprouts, nori pieces, green onions, and a sprinkle of sesame seeds.

9. Serve the tonkotsu ramen hot, allowing the flavors to meld together as you enjoy this comforting and hearty bowl of goodness.

Tonkotsu ramen is renowned for its rich and creamy broth, tender chashu pork, and delightful toppings.

The slow-cooked pork bones create a velvety base that's full of umami flavors.

Pair it with chewy ramen noodles and a variety of toppings for a satisfying and authentic ramen experience.

Customize your bowl with additional condiments like chili oil or garlic paste, and savor the harmonious blend of flavors in each spoonful.

Ii. Shoyu Ramen Recipe:

Ingredients:
- Chicken or vegetable broth (4 cups)
- Soy sauce (1/4 cup)
- Mirin (2 tablespoons)
- Ramen noodles (4 servings)
- Chashu pork or chicken slices (thinly sliced), or tofu cubes for a vegetarian option
- Soft-boiled eggs (1-2 per serving)
- Fresh spinach leaves, blanched (1 cup)
- Naruto fish cake slices (optional)
- Nori (seaweed) sheets, cut into small pieces
- Green onions, thinly sliced
- Sesame seeds, for garnish
- For the broth:
  - Ginger, sliced (2-inch piece)
  - Garlic cloves, minced (2-3 cloves)
  - Onion, sliced (1/2 medium onion)
  - Salt, to taste

Instructions:
1. In a large pot, combine the chicken or vegetable broth, soy sauce, mirin, ginger, garlic, onion, and a pinch of salt.

Bring the mixture to a boil and then reduce the heat to a simmer.

2. Allow the broth to simmer for about 20-30 minutes to infuse the flavors.

3. While the broth is simmering, cook the ramen noodles according to the package instructions.

Drain and rinse them with cold water to remove excess starch.

4. Once the broth is well-flavored, strain it through a fine-mesh sieve, discarding the solids.

Return the strained broth to the pot and keep it warm.

5. In a separate skillet, heat a small amount of oil and sauté the chashu pork or chicken slices until they are cooked through and slightly caramelized.

If using tofu, lightly pan-fry the tofu cubes until they are golden brown on all sides.

6. Divide the cooked ramen noodles among serving bowls.

Ladle the hot shoyu broth over the noodles, ensuring they are fully immersed.

7. Arrange the cooked chashu pork or chicken slices (or tofu cubes), soft-boiled eggs, blanched spinach leaves, Naruto fish cake slices, nori pieces, and green onions on top of the noodles.

8. Sprinkle sesame seeds over the bowls for garnish.

9. Serve the shoyu ramen hot and enjoy the harmonious blend of soy sauce-infused broth, tender proteins, and a variety of toppings.

Shoyu ramen is a classic Japanese dish known for its savory soy sauce-based broth and delightful toppings.

The combination of umami-rich flavors from the soy sauce and mirin creates a satisfying and well-balanced broth.

With tender chashu pork or chicken slices (or tofu for a vegetarian option), soft-boiled eggs, blanched spinach, and other toppings, this ramen offers a delightful variety of textures and flavors.

Enjoy the comforting and heartwarming experience of a bowl of shoyu ramen.

Iii. Miso Ramen Recipe:

Ingredients:
- Chicken or vegetable broth (4 cups)
- Miso paste (3-4 tablespoons)
- Soy sauce (2 tablespoons)
- Mirin (1 tablespoon)
- Ramen noodles (4 servings)
- Chashu pork or tofu cubes for a vegetarian option
- Soft-boiled eggs (1-2 per serving)
- Baby bok choy, halved (2-3 heads)
- Corn kernels (1/2 cup)
- Narutomaki fish cake slices (optional)
- Nori (seaweed) sheets, cut into small pieces
- Green onions, thinly sliced
- Sesame seeds, for garnish
- For the broth:
  - Ginger, sliced (1-inch piece)
  - Garlic cloves, minced (2-3 cloves)
  - Onion, sliced (1/2 medium onion)
  - Salt, to taste

Instructions:

1. In a large pot, combine the chicken or vegetable broth, miso paste, soy sauce, mirin, ginger, garlic, onion, and a pinch of salt. Bring the mixture to a gentle simmer.

2. Let the broth simmer for about 20-30 minutes to infuse the flavors.

3. While the broth is simmering, cook the ramen noodles according to the package instructions.

Drain and rinse them with cold water to remove excess starch.

4. Once the broth is well-flavored, strain it through a fine-mesh sieve, discarding the solids. Return the strained broth to the pot and keep it warm.

5. In a separate skillet, heat a small amount of oil and sauté the chashu pork or tofu cubes until they are cooked through and slightly caramelized.

6. Blanch the baby bok choy in boiling water for about 1-2 minutes until they are tender-crisp. Drain and set aside.

7. Divide the cooked ramen noodles among serving bowls. Ladle the hot miso broth over the noodles, ensuring they are fully immersed.

8. Arrange the cooked chashu pork or tofu cubes, soft-boiled eggs, blanched baby bok choy, corn kernels, narutomaki fish cake slices, nori pieces, and green onions on top of the noodles.

9. Sprinkle sesame seeds over the bowls for garnish.

10. Serve the miso ramen hot and savor the rich and savory flavors of the miso-infused broth, tender proteins, and a variety of toppings.

Miso ramen is a delightful variation of the classic Japanese ramen, featuring a flavorful broth made with miso paste.

The miso adds depth and umami to the broth, resulting in a rich and satisfying flavor profile.

With the addition of chashu pork or tofu, soft-boiled eggs, blanched baby bok choy, corn kernels, and other toppings, this ramen provides a combination of textures and tastes that will leave you craving for more.

Enjoy the comforting and delicious experience of a bowl of miso ramen.

iv. Spicy Tan Tan Ramen Recipe:

Ingredients:
- Chicken or vegetable broth (4 cups)
- Sesame paste or tahini (3 tablespoons)
- Soy sauce (2 tablespoons)
- Chili oil (1-2 tablespoons, adjust to desired spiciness)
- Garlic cloves, minced (2-3 cloves)
- Ginger, grated (1-inch piece)
- Ramen noodles (4 servings)
- Ground pork or tofu crumbles for a vegetarian option
- Soft-boiled eggs (1-2 per serving)
- Baby spinach leaves (1 cup)
- Green onions, thinly sliced
- Sesame seeds, for garnish
- For the broth:
  - Chicken or vegetable broth (1 cup)
  - Dried shiitake mushrooms (2-3 mushrooms)
  - Dried kelp (kombu) (1 small piece, about 2x2 inches)
  - Salt, to taste

Instructions:

1. In a medium pot, combine the chicken or vegetable broth, sesame paste or tahini, soy sauce, chili oil, minced garlic, grated ginger, and a pinch of salt.

Bring the mixture to a simmer and let it cook for about 10-15 minutes to allow the flavors to meld together.

2. While the broth is simmering, prepare the broth base by combining the additional cup of chicken or vegetable broth with the dried shiitake mushrooms and dried kelp in a separate pot.

Bring it to a gentle simmer and let it cook for about 10-15 minutes.

Remove the mushrooms and kelp and discard them. Set the broth aside.

3. Cook the ramen noodles according to the package instructions.

Drain and rinse them with cold water to remove excess starch.

4. In a skillet, heat a small amount of oil and cook the ground pork or tofu crumbles until they are browned and cooked through.

Set aside.

5. Add the prepared broth base to the main pot with the flavored broth and adjust the seasoning with salt if needed.

6. Divide the cooked ramen noodles among serving bowls.

Ladle the hot spicy tan tan broth over the noodles, ensuring they are fully immersed.

7. Top the bowls with the cooked ground pork or tofu crumbles, soft-boiled eggs, baby spinach leaves, and sliced green onions.

8. Sprinkle sesame seeds over the bowls for garnish.

9. Serve the spicy tan tan ramen hot and relish the bold and spicy flavors of the sesame-infused broth, combined with the hearty protein, fresh greens, and aromatic toppings.

Spicy Tan Tan Ramen is a fiery and flavorful variation of Japanese ramen.

The combination of sesame paste, soy sauce, and chili oil creates a deliciously spicy and nutty broth.

With the addition of ground pork or tofu, soft-boiled eggs, baby spinach leaves, and other toppings, this ramen offers a delightful contrast of textures and flavors.

Enjoy the satisfying heat and rich aromas of a bowl of spicy tan tan ramen.

Section 3: Thai Curry and Noodles

- Introduction to Thai Cuisine:

Thai cuisine is renowned for its vibrant flavors, aromatic herbs, and skillful balance of sweet, sour, spicy, and savory elements.

With its diverse range of ingredients and regional variations,

Thai cuisine offers a delightful culinary journey for food enthusiasts.

From fragrant curries to noodles dishes bursting with flavors,

Thai cuisine is a treasure trove of culinary delights.

Thai cuisine is deeply influenced by the country's geography and cultural history.

The use of fresh herbs and spices, such as lemongrass, galangal, lime leaves, and Thai basil, adds distinct flavors and aromas to the dishes.

The combination of these ingredients with staples like rice, noodles, coconut milk, and fish sauce creates a unique culinary experience that is both satisfying and complex.

In Thai cuisine, the balance of flavors is crucial.

The dishes often incorporate the four main taste components: sweet, sour, spicy, and salty.

This balance is achieved through the skillful use of ingredients like palm sugar, lime juice, chili peppers, and fish sauce.

Whether it's a creamy and fragrant curry or a tangy and refreshing salad, Thai cuisine excels in creating harmonious flavor profiles that tantalize the taste buds.

One of the defining features of Thai cuisine is the extensive use of fresh herbs and vegetables.

Thai dishes are often garnished with cilantro, Thai basil, mint, and scallions, which add freshness and visual appeal to the plate.

Additionally, the use of aromatic pastes and sauces, such as red, green, or yellow curry pastes, tamarind sauce, and peanut sauce, adds depth and complexity to the dishes.

In the following sections, we will explore some of the iconic dishes from Thai cuisine.

From fragrant curries like green curry and massaman curry to noodle dishes like pad Thai and drunken noodles, we will embark on a culinary adventure through the diverse and exciting flavors of Thai cuisine.

Fragrant Thai Curries:

Thai curries are known for their rich, aromatic flavors and luscious coconut milk-based sauces.

These curries are a staple in Thai cuisine and offer a delightful blend of spices, herbs, and creamy textures.

From mild and fragrant to fiery and intense,

Thai curries cater to a range of taste preferences and are beloved by food enthusiasts worldwide.

The base of Thai curries is a paste made from a combination of fresh herbs, spices, and aromatics.

The most common Thai curry pastes include red, green, and yellow, each offering a distinct flavor profile.

These pastes typically consist of ingredients like lemongrass, galangal, Thai chilies, garlic, shallots, and a variety of spices.

The paste is sautéed in oil to release its flavors before being combined with coconut milk and other ingredients.

Thai curries are versatile and can be made with a variety of proteins and vegetables.

From succulent chicken and tender beef to fresh seafood and vegetarian options, the choice of ingredients allows for endless possibilities.

The combination of flavors and textures in Thai curries is enhanced by the addition of vegetables like bell peppers, bamboo shoots, Thai eggplant, and herbs like Thai basil and kaffir lime leaves.

Now let's dive into the first recipe of this section:

i. Green Curry Recipe:

Ingredients:
- Green curry paste (3 tablespoons)
- Coconut milk (1 can)
- Chicken or your choice of protein, sliced (8-10 ounces)
- Thai eggplant, cut into wedges (1 cup)
- Bamboo shoots, sliced (1/2 cup)
- Kaffir lime leaves, torn (4-5 leaves)
- Thai basil leaves, torn (1/4 cup)
- Fish sauce (1 tablespoon)
- Palm sugar or brown sugar (1 teaspoon)
- Vegetable oil (2 tablespoons)

Instructions:
1. Heat vegetable oil in a large skillet or wok over medium heat. Add green curry paste and stir-fry for a minute until fragrant.

2. Pour in half of the coconut milk (the thick, creamy part) and stir well with the curry paste until combined.

3. Add the chicken or protein of your choice to the skillet and cook until it is almost cooked through.

4. Add the remaining coconut milk and bring the mixture to a simmer.

5. Add Thai eggplant, bamboo shoots, kaffir lime leaves, fish sauce, and palm sugar. Stir well to combine.

6. Simmer the curry for about 10-15 minutes until the flavors meld together and the chicken is cooked through.

7. Taste and adjust the seasoning if needed, adding more fish sauce for saltiness or sugar for sweetness.

8. Remove the curry from heat and stir in the torn Thai basil leaves.

9. Serve the green curry hot with steamed jasmine rice or noodles, garnishing with additional Thai basil leaves if desired.

Green curry is a classic Thai dish known for its vibrant green color and aromatic flavors.

The combination of the fragrant green curry paste, creamy coconut milk, and a variety of vegetables and proteins creates a harmonious balance of spicy, savory, and sweet flavors.

Enjoy the fragrant aroma and comforting warmth of this delightful Thai green curry.

ii. Recipe: Red Curry

Red curry is another popular and flavorful Thai curry that offers a perfect balance of spicy and aromatic flavors.

Made with a vibrant red curry paste and creamy coconut milk, this curry is known for its rich and comforting taste.

It showcases the depth and complexity of Thai cuisine, with its combination of herbs, spices, and carefully selected ingredients.

Recipe for Red Curry:

Ingredients:
- Red curry paste (3 tablespoons)
- Coconut milk (1 can)
- Chicken or your choice of protein, sliced (8-10 ounces)
- Red bell pepper, sliced (1 medium)
- Bamboo shoots, sliced (1/2 cup)
- Thai basil leaves, torn (1/4 cup)
- Fish sauce (1 tablespoon)
- Palm sugar or brown sugar (1 teaspoon)
- Vegetable oil (2 tablespoons)

Instructions:
1. Heat vegetable oil in a large skillet or wok over medium heat. Add the red curry paste and stir-fry for a minute until fragrant.

2. Pour in half of the coconut milk (the thick, creamy part) and stir well with the curry paste until combined.

3. Add the chicken or protein of your choice to the skillet and cook until it is almost cooked through.

4. Add the remaining coconut milk and bring the mixture to a simmer.

5. Add red bell pepper and bamboo shoots to the curry. Stir well to combine.

6. Add fish sauce and palm sugar, adjusting the amount to your taste preferences.

7. Simmer the curry for about 10-15 minutes, allowing the flavors to meld together and the chicken to cook through.

8. Taste and adjust the seasoning if needed, adding more fish sauce for saltiness or sugar for sweetness.

9. Remove the curry from heat and stir in the torn Thai basil leaves.
10. Serve the red curry hot with steamed jasmine rice or noodles, garnishing with additional Thai basil leaves if desired.

Red curry is known for its robust and spicy flavors, with the red curry paste adding a depth of heat and complexity to the dish.

The combination of creamy coconut milk, tender chicken or protein, and the vibrant vegetables creates a satisfying and aromatic curry that is sure to delight your taste buds.

iii. Recipe: Massaman Curry:

Massaman curry is a unique and rich Thai curry that combines the flavors of Thailand with influences from Indian and Middle Eastern cuisines.

This curry is known for its complex and aromatic taste, featuring a combination of spices, tender meat, creamy coconut milk, and a hint of sweetness.

It is a true culinary masterpiece that showcases the fusion of flavors in Thai cuisine.

Recipe for Massaman Curry:

Ingredients:
- Massaman curry paste (3 tablespoons)

- Coconut milk (1 can)
- Beef, chicken, or your choice of protein, cut into bite-sized pieces (8-10 ounces)
- Potatoes, peeled and cubed (2 medium)
- Onion, sliced (1 medium)
- Roasted peanuts, crushed (1/4 cup)
- Cinnamon stick (1)
- Bay leaves (2)
- Fish sauce (1 tablespoon)
- Tamarind paste (1 tablespoon)
- Palm sugar or brown sugar (1 teaspoon)
- Vegetable oil (2 tablespoons)

Instructions:

1. Heat vegetable oil in a large skillet or wok over medium heat. Add the Massaman curry paste and stir-fry for a minute until fragrant.

2. Pour in half of the coconut milk (the thick, creamy part) and stir well with the curry paste until combined.

3. Add the beef, chicken, or protein of your choice to the skillet and cook until it is browned on all sides.

4. Add the remaining coconut milk and bring the mixture to a simmer.

5. Add the potatoes, onion, crushed peanuts, cinnamon stick, and bay leaves to the curry. Stir well to combine.

6. Add fish sauce, tamarind paste, and palm sugar, adjusting the amounts to your taste preferences.

7. Simmer the curry for about 30-40 minutes, or until the meat is tender and the potatoes are cooked through.

8. Taste and adjust the seasoning if needed, adding more fish sauce, tamarind paste, or sugar as desired.

9. Remove the cinnamon stick and bay leaves from the curry before serving.

10. Serve the Massaman curry hot with steamed jasmine rice or Thai-style roti bread.

Massaman curry is known for its distinctive flavor profile, with a harmonious blend of fragrant spices, creamy coconut milk, and tender meat.

The addition of potatoes and peanuts adds a delightful texture to the dish, while the sweetness from the palm sugar and the tanginess from the tamarind paste create a well-rounded flavor experience.

Iv. Panang Curry Recipe:

Panang curry is a popular Thai curry known for its rich and creamy texture, along with its slightly sweet and nutty flavor profile.

It is a milder and less spicy curry compared to other Thai curries, making it a favorite among those who prefer a milder heat.

The combination of aromatic herbs, spices, and coconut milk creates a delightful and satisfying dish that is sure to please your taste buds.

Recipe for Panang Curry:

Ingredients:
- Panang curry paste (3 tablespoons)
- Coconut milk (1 can)
- Chicken, beef, or your choice of protein, sliced (8-10 ounces)
- Kaffir lime leaves, torn (4-5 leaves)
- Thai basil leaves, torn (1/4 cup)

- Red bell pepper, sliced (1 medium)
- Fish sauce (1 tablespoon)
- Palm sugar or brown sugar (1 teaspoon)
- Vegetable oil (2 tablespoons)

Instructions:
1. Heat vegetable oil in a large skillet or wok over medium heat. Add the Panang curry paste and stir-fry for a minute until fragrant.

2. Pour in half of the coconut milk (the thick, creamy part) and stir well with the curry paste until combined.

3. Add the chicken, beef, or protein of your choice to the skillet and cook until it is almost cooked through.

4. Add the remaining coconut milk and bring the mixture to a simmer.

5. Add kaffir lime leaves, Thai basil leaves, and red bell pepper to the curry. Stir well to combine.

6. Add fish sauce and palm sugar, adjusting the amounts to your taste preferences.

7. Simmer the curry for about 10-15 minutes, allowing the flavors to meld together and the meat to cook through.

8. Taste and adjust the seasoning if needed, adding more fish sauce or sugar as desired.

9. Remove the curry from heat and serve it hot with steamed jasmine rice.

Panang curry is known for its velvety texture, creamy coconut undertones, and the aromatic combination of herbs and spices.

The addition of kaffir lime leaves and Thai basil adds a refreshing and vibrant element to the dish, while the red bell pepper provides a slight crunch and sweetness.

Delectable Thai Noodles:

Thai cuisine is renowned for its wide variety of noodle dishes that are bursting with flavors and textures.

From stir-fried noodles to soups, Thai noodles offer a delightful combination of savory, sweet, sour, and spicy tastes.

These dishes showcase the versatility of noodles and the art of balancing flavors in Thai cooking.

i. Pad Thai Recipe:

Ingredients:
- Rice noodles (8 ounces)
- Shrimp, chicken, or tofu, cooked and sliced (8-10 ounces)
- Bean sprouts (1 cup)
- Garlic, minced (3 cloves)
- Shallots, thinly sliced (2)
- Eggs, beaten (2)
- Tamarind paste (3 tablespoons)
- Fish sauce (2 tablespoons)
- Palm sugar or brown sugar (2 tablespoons)
- Crushed peanuts (1/4 cup)
- Lime wedges, for serving
- Fresh cilantro, for garnish
- Vegetable oil (2 tablespoons)

Instructions:

1. Soak the rice noodles in warm water for about 15-20 minutes until they are soft and pliable. Drain and set aside.

2. Heat vegetable oil in a large skillet or wok over medium heat. Add the minced garlic and sliced shallots, and stir-fry for a minute until fragrant.

3. Push the garlic and shallots to one side of the skillet, and pour the beaten eggs into the other side. Scramble the eggs until they are partially cooked.

4. Add the shrimp, chicken, or tofu to the skillet and cook until they are almost done.

5. Add the soaked rice noodles to the skillet and stir-fry for a few minutes until they are coated with the ingredients.

6. In a small bowl, mix together tamarind paste, fish sauce, and palm sugar until the sugar is dissolved.

Pour the sauce mixture over the noodles and stir well to combine.

7. Add the bean sprouts to the skillet and toss everything together. Cook for a few more minutes until the noodles are heated through.

8. Sprinkle crushed peanuts over the noodles and give them a final toss.

9. Serve the Pad Thai hot, garnished with fresh cilantro and lime wedges on the side.

Pad Thai is one of the most iconic Thai noodle dishes, known for its balance of sweet, tangy, and savory flavors.

The combination of rice noodles, protein, bean sprouts, crushed peanuts, and aromatic ingredients creates a harmonious dish that is both satisfying and refreshing.

ii. Recipe: Pad See Ew:

Pad See Ew is a popular Thai noodle dish that is loved for its rich and savory flavors.

Made with wide rice noodles stir-fried with soy sauce, vegetables, and your choice of protein, Pad See Ew is a comforting and satisfying dish that is enjoyed by both locals and visitors alike.

Recipe: Pad See Ew:

Ingredients:
- Wide rice noodles (8 ounces)
- Chicken, beef, or tofu, sliced (8-10 ounces)
- Broccoli florets (1 cup)
- Carrots, sliced (1/2 cup)
- Chinese broccoli or kale, chopped (1 cup)
- Garlic, minced (3 cloves)
- Eggs, beaten (2)
- Dark soy sauce (3 tablespoons)
- Oyster sauce (2 tablespoons)
- Fish sauce (1 tablespoon)
- Vegetable oil (2 tablespoons)

Instructions:
1. Cook the wide rice noodles according to the package instructions. Drain and set aside.

2. Heat vegetable oil in a large skillet or wok over medium heat. Add the minced garlic and stir-fry for a minute until fragrant.

3. Push the garlic to one side of the skillet, and pour the beaten eggs into the other side. Scramble the eggs until they are partially cooked.

4. Add the chicken, beef, or tofu to the skillet and cook until they are almost done.

5. Add the broccoli florets, sliced carrots, and Chinese broccoli or kale to the skillet. Stir-fry the vegetables until they are tender-crisp.

6. Add the cooked rice noodles to the skillet and toss everything together.

7. In a small bowl, mix together dark soy sauce, oyster sauce, and fish sauce. Pour the sauce mixture over the noodles and stir well to combine.

8. Continue stir-frying for a few more minutes until the noodles are evenly coated with the sauce and everything is heated through.

9. Taste and adjust the seasoning if needed, adding more soy sauce or fish sauce according to your preference.

10. Serve the Pad See Ew hot, garnished with a sprinkle of fresh cilantro or sliced green onions.

Pad See Ew showcases the art of stir-frying, where the flavors of the ingredients are enhanced by the caramelization process.

The combination of wide rice noodles, tender protein, crisp vegetables, and the umami-rich sauce creates a harmonious and comforting dish that is enjoyed by noodle lovers everywhere.

ii. Drunken Noodles (Pad Kee Mao):

Drunken Noodles, also known as Pad Kee Mao, is a popular Thai dish known for its bold and spicy flavors.

Despite its name, the dish does not contain any alcohol .

This stir-fried noodle dish is packed with aromatic ingredients, fresh herbs, and a delightful blend of savory and spicy sauces.

Recipe: Drunken Noodles (Pad Kee Mao):

Ingredients:
- Wide rice noodles (8 ounces)
- Chicken, beef, shrimp, or tofu, sliced (8-10 ounces)
- Bell peppers, sliced (1-2)
- Thai chili peppers, sliced (2-3)
- Garlic, minced (3 cloves)
- Thai basil leaves (1/2 cup)
- Fish sauce (2 tablespoons)
- Oyster sauce (2 tablespoons)
- Soy sauce (1 tablespoon)
- Sugar (1 teaspoon)
- Vegetable oil (2 tablespoons)

Instructions:
1. Cook the wide rice noodles according to the package instructions. Drain and set aside.

2. Heat vegetable oil in a large skillet or wok over medium heat. Add the minced garlic and sliced Thai chili peppers. Stir-fry for a minute until fragrant.

3. Add the sliced chicken, beef, shrimp, or tofu to the skillet and cook until they are almost done.

4. Add the sliced bell peppers to the skillet and stir-fry for a few minutes until they are slightly tender.

5. Push the ingredients to one side of the skillet, creating an empty space. Crack the eggs into the empty space and scramble them until they are partially cooked.

6. Add the cooked rice noodles to the skillet and toss everything together.

7. In a small bowl, mix together fish sauce, oyster sauce, soy sauce, and sugar. Pour the sauce mixture over the noodles and stir well to combine.

8. Continue stir-frying for a few more minutes until the noodles are evenly coated with the sauce and everything is heated through.

9. Add Thai basil leaves to the skillet and toss them with the noodles until they are wilted.

10. Taste and adjust the seasoning if needed, adding more fish sauce or sugar according to your preference.

11. Serve the Drunken Noodles hot, garnished with extra Thai basil leaves and sliced Thai chili peppers for an extra kick.

Drunken Noodles (Pad Kee Mao) is a delightful combination of wide rice noodles, tender protein, vibrant vegetables, and aromatic herbs.

The spicy and savory flavors of the dish make it a favorite among Thai food enthusiasts who enjoy a little heat in their meals.

iii. Tom Yum Noodle Soup:

Tom Yum Noodle Soup is a popular Thai soup known for its bold and tangy flavors.

This hot and sour soup is made with a fragrant broth infused with lemongrass, kaffir lime leaves, and Thai chilies, and it is packed with tender noodles, succulent shrimp or chicken, and a variety of fresh herbs and vegetables.

It's a perfect balance of spicy, sour, and savory flavors.

Recipe: Tom Yum Noodle Soup:

Ingredients:
- Rice noodles (8 ounces)
- Shrimp or chicken, peeled and deveined (8-10 ounces)
- Mushrooms, sliced (1 cup)
- Tomatoes, diced (1/2 cup)
- Lemongrass stalk, bruised (1)
- Kaffir lime leaves (3-4)
- Thai chilies, sliced (2-3)
- Galangal or ginger, sliced (1-inch piece)
- Garlic, minced (3 cloves)
- Fish sauce (3 tablespoons)
- Lime juice (2 tablespoons)
- Sugar (1 teaspoon)
- Vegetable oil (2 tablespoons)
- Fresh cilantro, chopped (for garnish)
- Green onions, sliced (for garnish)

Instructions:
1. Cook the rice noodles according to the package instructions. Drain and set aside.

2. In a large pot, heat vegetable oil over medium heat.

Add the minced garlic, sliced Thai chilies, and sliced galangal or ginger.

Stir-fry for a minute until fragrant.

3. Add the shrimp or chicken to the pot and cook until they are almost done.

4. Pour in enough water to cover the ingredients in the pot.

Add the bruised lemongrass stalk, kaffir lime leaves, and mushrooms.

Bring the mixture to a simmer and let it cook for about 10 minutes to allow the flavors to meld.

5. Add the diced tomatoes to the pot and continue simmering for another 5 minutes until the tomatoes are slightly softened.

6. Stir in the fish sauce, lime juice, and sugar.

Taste the broth and adjust the seasoning according to your preference, adding more fish sauce for saltiness or more lime juice for acidity.

7. To serve, place a portion of cooked rice noodles in a bowl.

Ladle the hot soup over the noodles, making sure to include the shrimp or chicken, mushrooms, and tomatoes.

8. Garnish the soup with fresh cilantro and sliced green onions for added freshness and aroma.

9. Serve the Tom Yum Noodle Soup hot and enjoy its vibrant flavors.

Tom Yum Noodle Soup is a comforting and satisfying dish that showcases the complexity of Thai flavors.

The aromatic broth combined with the tender noodles and succulent shrimp or chicken creates a soup that is both soothing and invigorating, making it a beloved choice among Thai food lovers.

Section 4: Indian Spices and Curries

- Introduction to Indian Cuisine:

Indian cuisine is renowned for its rich flavors, vibrant spices, and diverse range of dishes.

With its vast culinary traditions and regional variations, Indian cuisine offers a delightful journey for the taste buds.

From aromatic curries to flavorful rice dishes and delectable breads, the use of spices and herbs plays a central role in Indian cooking, creating a tapestry of complex and tantalizing flavors.

In this section, we will explore the essence of Indian cuisine, its key ingredients, and the art of creating traditional Indian curries.

From mild and creamy to fiery and robust, Indian curries span a wide spectrum of flavors and styles, allowing you to experience the diverse regional tastes of India.

Get ready to embark on a culinary adventure through the tantalizing world of Indian spices and curries.

Flavorful Indian Curries:

Indian cuisine is synonymous with its aromatic and flavorful curries.

These rich and diverse dishes are the heart and soul of Indian cooking, showcasing a perfect balance of spices, herbs, and ingredients.

From creamy and mild to fiery and robust, Indian curries are a delightful amalgamation of flavors that vary across different regions of the country.

Whether you're a fan of vegetarian curries or enjoy indulging in meat-based dishes, Indian cuisine offers a wide range of options to satisfy every palate.

i. Recipe: Butter Chicken

Butter Chicken, also known as Murgh Makhani, is a popular Indian curry that originated in the northern part of the country.

It is a creamy and indulgent dish made with tender chicken pieces simmered in a rich tomato-based gravy.

The sauce is luscious and buttery, with a perfect balance of sweetness and tanginess.

Butter Chicken is best enjoyed with steamed basmati rice or freshly baked naan bread.

Ingredients:
- Chicken, boneless and skinless, cut into pieces (1.5 pounds)
- Yogurt, plain and thick (1/2 cup)
- Ginger-garlic paste (1 tablespoon)
- Kashmiri red chili powder (1 teaspoon)
- Garam masala (1 teaspoon)
- Turmeric powder (1/2 teaspoon)
- Salt, to taste
- Butter (4 tablespoons)
- Oil (2 tablespoons)
- Onion, finely chopped (1 medium-sized)

- Tomatoes, pureed (2 large)
- Cashew nuts, soaked in warm water (10-12)
- Heavy cream (1/2 cup)
- Kasuri methi (dried fenugreek leaves), crushed (1 tablespoon)
- Fresh cilantro leaves, chopped (for garnish)

Instructions:
1. In a bowl, combine the yogurt, ginger-garlic paste, Kashmiri red chili powder, garam masala, turmeric powder, and salt. Mix well to form a marinade.

2. Add the chicken pieces to the marinade, ensuring they are well-coated.

 Allow the chicken to marinate for at least 30 minutes or up to overnight in the refrigerator.

3. Heat butter and oil in a large pan or skillet over medium heat.

Add the chopped onions and sauté until they turn golden brown.

4. Add the pureed tomatoes to the pan and cook for a few minutes until the oil starts to separate from the mixture.

5. Drain the soaked cashew nuts and add them to a blender.

Blend until you get a smooth paste. Add the cashew paste to the pan and cook for another couple of minutes.

6. Add the marinated chicken along with the marinade to the pan.

Cook over medium heat, stirring occasionally, until the chicken is cooked through and tender.

7. Stir in the heavy cream and kasuri methi.

Simmer the curry for a few more minutes to allow the flavors to meld together.

8. Taste the curry and adjust the seasoning if needed, adding more salt or spices according to your preference.

9. Garnish with freshly chopped cilantro leaves before serving.

10. Serve Butter Chicken hot with steamed basmati rice or naan bread.

Butter Chicken is a true indulgence in Indian cuisine, with its velvety smooth sauce and tender chicken that melts in your mouth.

The combination of aromatic spices and rich flavors makes it a favorite choice among curry lovers worldwide.

ii. Recipe: Lamb Rogan Josh

Ingredients:
- Lamb, bone-in, cut into pieces (1.5 pounds)
- Yogurt, plain and thick (1/2 cup)
- Ginger-garlic paste (1 tablespoon)
- Kashmiri red chili powder (1 teaspoon)
- Ground cumin (1 teaspoon)
- Ground coriander (1 teaspoon)
- Turmeric powder (1/2 teaspoon)
- Salt, to taste
- Oil (3 tablespoons)
- Cinnamon stick (1 inch)
- Green cardamom pods (4)
- Cloves (4)
- Bay leaf (1)
- Onion, finely chopped (1 large)
- Tomatoes, pureed (2 medium-sized)

- Tomato paste (1 tablespoon)
- Fennel powder (1/2 teaspoon)
- Garam masala (1/2 teaspoon)
- Fresh cilantro leaves, chopped (for garnish)

Instructions:
1. In a bowl, combine the yogurt, ginger-garlic paste, Kashmiri red chili powder, ground cumin, ground coriander, turmeric powder, and salt.

Mix well to form a marinade.

2. Add the lamb pieces to the marinade, ensuring they are well-coated.

 Allow the lamb to marinate for at least 1 hour or refrigerate overnight for best results.

3. Heat oil in a large pot or Dutch oven over medium heat.

Add the cinnamon stick, cardamom pods, cloves, and bay leaf. Sauté for a minute until fragrant.

4. Add the chopped onions to the pot and sauté until they turn golden brown.

5. Add the pureed tomatoes and tomato paste to the pot.

Cook for a few minutes until the oil starts to separate from the mixture.

6. Add the marinated lamb along with the marinade to the pot.

Stir well to coat the lamb with the tomato mixture.

7. Reduce the heat to low, cover the pot, and simmer for about 1.5 to 2 hours, or until the lamb is tender and the flavors have melded together.

Stir occasionally to prevent sticking.

8. Sprinkle fennel powder and garam masala over the curry.

Stir well to incorporate the spices.

9. Taste the curry and adjust the seasoning if needed, adding more salt or spices according to your preference.

10. Garnish with freshly chopped cilantro leaves before serving.

11. Serve Lamb Rogan Josh hot with steamed basmati rice or naan bread.

Lamb Rogan Josh is a classic Indian curry that hails from the region of Kashmir.

It is known for its rich and aromatic flavors, with tender lamb simmered in a fragrant tomato-based sauce.

The combination of spices, including Kashmiri red chili powder and garam masala, gives the curry its signature deep red color and robust taste.

Enjoy this indulgent dish that showcases the essence of Indian cuisine.

iii. Recipe: Chana Masala (Chickpea Curry)

Ingredients:

- Chickpeas, cooked or canned (2 cups)
- Onion, finely chopped (1 large)
- Garlic cloves, minced (3)
- Ginger, grated (1-inch piece)
- Green chili, finely chopped (1)
- Tomatoes, pureed (2 medium-sized)
- Tomato paste (2 tablespoons)
- Ground cumin (1 teaspoon)
- Ground coriander (1 teaspoon)
- Turmeric powder (1/2 teaspoon)
- Red chili powder (1/2 teaspoon)
- Garam masala (1/2 teaspoon)
- Salt, to taste
- Oil (2 tablespoons)
- Fresh cilantro leaves, chopped (for garnish)

Instructions:
1. Heat oil in a large pan or skillet over medium heat.

2. Add the chopped onions and sauté until they turn golden brown.

3. Add minced garlic, grated ginger, and green chili to the pan. Sauté for another minute until fragrant.

4. Add the pureed tomatoes and tomato paste to the pan. Cook for a few minutes until the oil starts to separate from the mixture.

5. Stir in the ground cumin, ground coriander, turmeric powder, red chili powder, and salt. Cook for a minute to toast the spices and enhance their flavors.

6. Add the cooked or canned chickpeas to the pan. Stir well to coat the chickpeas with the tomato and spice mixture.

7. Reduce the heat to low, cover the pan, and simmer for about 15-20 minutes, allowing the flavors to meld together.

8. Sprinkle garam masala over the curry. Stir well to incorporate the spice.

9. Taste the curry and adjust the seasoning if needed, adding more salt or spices according to your preference.

10. Garnish with freshly chopped cilantro leaves before serving.

11. Serve Chana Masala hot with steamed basmati rice or naan bread.

Chana Masala, also known as Chickpea Curry, is a popular vegetarian dish in Indian cuisine.

It is made with tender chickpeas cooked in a rich and flavorful tomato-based sauce.

The combination of aromatic spices gives this curry its distinct taste and aroma.

Chana Masala is not only delicious but also a great source of plant-based protein and fiber.

Enjoy this hearty and satisfying dish that showcases the vibrant flavors of Indian spices.

iv. Recipe: Palak Paneer (Spinach and Cottage Cheese Curry)

Ingredients:
- Spinach, fresh or frozen (2 cups)
- Paneer (cottage cheese), cubed (200 grams)
- Onion, finely chopped (1 medium-sized)
- Garlic cloves, minced (2)
- Ginger, grated (1-inch piece)
- Green chili, finely chopped (1)

- Tomatoes, pureed (2 medium-sized)
- Ground cumin (1 teaspoon)
- Ground coriander (1 teaspoon)
- Turmeric powder (1/2 teaspoon)
- Red chili powder (1/2 teaspoon)
- Garam masala (1/2 teaspoon)
- Salt, to taste
- Oil (2 tablespoons)
- Fresh cream (optional, for garnish)
- Fresh cilantro leaves, chopped (for garnish)

Instructions:
1. Wash the spinach leaves thoroughly and blanch them in boiling water for 2-3 minutes.

Drain and transfer to a bowl of ice water to retain their vibrant green color.
Once cooled, drain again and blend the spinach to a smooth puree.

Set aside.

2. Heat oil in a large pan or skillet over medium heat.

3. Add the chopped onions and sauté until they turn translucent.

4. Add minced garlic, grated ginger, and green chili to the pan.
Sauté for another minute until fragrant.

5. Add the pureed tomatoes to the pan. Cook for a few minutes until the oil starts to separate from the mixture.

6. Stir in the ground cumin, ground coriander, turmeric powder, red chili powder, and salt.

Cook for a minute to toast the spices and enhance their flavors.

7. Add the spinach puree to the pan. Mix well with the tomato and spice mixture.

8. Gently place the paneer cubes into the pan.

Stir gently to coat the paneer with the spinach curry.

9. Reduce the heat to low, cover the pan, and simmer for about 10-15 minutes to allow the flavors to blend together and the paneer to absorb the curry.

10. Sprinkle garam masala over the curry. Stir gently to incorporate the spice.

11. Taste the curry and adjust the seasoning if needed, adding more salt or spices according to your preference.

12. Garnish with a drizzle of fresh cream (optional) and freshly chopped cilantro leaves before serving.

13. Serve Palak Paneer hot with naan bread or steamed basmati rice.

Palak Paneer is a popular vegetarian dish in Indian cuisine, where paneer (cottage cheese) is cooked in a creamy spinach curry.

This vibrant and nutritious dish is not only visually appealing but also packed with flavor.

The combination of fresh spinach, aromatic spices, and soft paneer creates a delightful and comforting meal.

Enjoy the richness of Palak Paneer and savor the taste of Indian spices.

Fragrant Indian Spices:

Indian cuisine is renowned for its vibrant and aromatic spices that lend distinct flavors to the dishes.

The combination of these spices creates a symphony of taste, taking your culinary experience to new heights.

From earthy cumin to warm coriander, pungent turmeric to fiery chili powder, each spice has its unique role in Indian cooking.

The skillful use of these spices can transform a simple dish into a flavorful masterpiece.

Garam Masala:

Garam Masala is a quintessential spice blend used in Indian cooking. The name "garam" translates to "hot," but it refers to the warmth and depth of flavor rather than spiciness.

This aromatic blend typically consists of a mixture of ground spices such as cinnamon, cardamom, cloves, cumin, coriander, and black pepper.

The exact composition may vary depending on regional preferences and family recipes.

Recipe: Garam Masala

Ingredients:
- Cumin seeds (2 tablespoons)
- Coriander seeds (2 tablespoons)
- Green cardamom pods (10)

- Whole cloves (1 tablespoon)
- Cinnamon stick (1-inch piece)
- Black peppercorns (1 teaspoon)
- Nutmeg, grated (1/2 teaspoon, optional)

Instructions:
1. Heat a dry skillet over medium heat and add the cumin seeds, coriander seeds, cardamom pods, cloves, cinnamon stick, and black peppercorns.

2. Toast the spices for a few minutes until they become fragrant, stirring continuously to prevent burning.

3. Remove the skillet from heat and allow the spices to cool completely.

4. Transfer the cooled spices to a spice grinder or mortar and pestle.

5. Grind the spices into a fine powder.

6. If using, grate the nutmeg and add it to the ground spice blend.

Mix well.

7. Store the homemade Garam Masala in an airtight container in a cool, dry place.

Garam Masala adds a rich and aromatic flavor to a variety of Indian dishes.

It is often added towards the end of cooking or used as a finishing spice to enhance the taste and aroma of curries, stews, and even rice dishes.

With its warm and complex flavor profile, Garam Masala is a staple in Indian cuisine and a delightful addition to your spice collection.

Curry Powder:

Curry powder is a versatile spice blend commonly used in Indian and Southeast Asian cuisines.

It is a combination of various ground spices that varies depending on regional preferences and family recipes.

While the exact composition can differ, curry powder typically includes a blend of aromatic spices such as turmeric, coriander, cumin, fenugreek, cinnamon, cardamom, cloves, and black pepper.

The resulting mixture creates a complex and flavorful spice blend that adds depth and warmth to a wide range of dishes.

Recipe: Curry Powder

Ingredients:
- Turmeric powder (4 tablespoons)
- Coriander powder (2 tablespoons)
- Cumin powder (2 tablespoons)
- Fenugreek powder (1 tablespoon)
- Cinnamon powder (1 tablespoon)
- Cardamom powder (1 tablespoon)
- Clove powder (1 tablespoon)
- Black pepper powder (1 tablespoon)

Instructions:
1. In a mixing bowl, combine all the spice powders: turmeric, coriander, cumin, fenugreek, cinnamon, cardamom, cloves, and black pepper.

2. Mix well until the spices are thoroughly combined.

3. Transfer the curry powder to an airtight container for storage.

4. Store in a cool, dry place away from direct sunlight.

Curry powder serves as a convenient way to introduce a blend of flavors and spices into your cooking.

It can be used as a base for various curry dishes, marinades, spice rubs, and even in soups and stews.

The vibrant yellow color from turmeric gives curry powder its characteristic appearance, while the combination of aromatic spices provides a delightful aroma and taste.

Remember, while store-bought curry powder is readily available, making your own allows you to customize the blend to suit your preferences and experiment with different ratios of spices.

Feel free to adjust the proportions of the spices in the recipe to achieve your desired flavor profile.

Tandoori Masala:

Tandoori Masala is a vibrant spice blend that is widely used in Indian cuisine, particularly in the preparation of tandoori-style dishes.

It gets its name from the traditional clay oven called a tandoor, where these dishes are traditionally cooked.

Tandoori Masala is known for its bold flavors and fiery red color, which comes from the inclusion of ground red chili peppers.

Recipe: Tandoori Masala

Ingredients:
- Paprika (4 tablespoons)
- Ground coriander (2 tablespoons)
- Ground cumin (2 tablespoons)
- Ground turmeric (1 tablespoon)
- Ground ginger (1 tablespoon)
- Ground cinnamon (1 teaspoon)
- Ground cloves (1 teaspoon)
- Ground nutmeg (1/2 teaspoon)
- Ground cardamom (1/2 teaspoon)
- Ground black pepper (1/2 teaspoon)
- Ground red chili powder (adjust to desired level of spiciness)

Instructions:
1. In a mixing bowl, combine all the spice powders: paprika, ground coriander, ground cumin, ground turmeric, ground ginger, ground cinnamon, ground cloves, ground nutmeg, ground cardamom, ground black pepper, and ground red chili powder.

2. Mix well until all the spices are thoroughly combined.

3. Transfer the Tandoori Masala to an airtight container for storage.

4. Store in a cool, dry place away from direct sunlight.

Tandoori Masala is most commonly used as a marinade for meats, such as chicken, lamb, or fish.

The spice blend, when mixed with yogurt or lime juice, creates a flavorful paste that infuses the meat with a distinct smoky and tangy taste.

The vibrant red color achieved from the red chili powder gives tandoori dishes their appetizing appearance.

Apart from marinating meats, Tandoori Masala can also be used as a seasoning in various other dishes, such as roasted vegetables, grilled paneer (Indian cottage cheese), or even as a sprinkle over snacks like roasted chickpeas or popcorn.

Feel free to adjust the spice levels in the Tandoori Masala recipe to suit your personal taste preferences.

Experimenting with different ratios of spices allows you to create a custom blend that caters to your desired level of heat and flavor intensity.

Rasam Powder:

Rasam Powder is a traditional South Indian spice blend that is essential for making rasam, a tangy and flavorful soup.

 Rasam is a popular dish in South Indian cuisine and is typically served with rice or enjoyed as a soup on its own.

 Rasam Powder adds a distinctive aroma and a well-balanced combination of spices to the dish.

Recipe: Rasam Powder

Ingredients:
- Coriander seeds (4 tablespoons)
- Cumin seeds (2 tablespoons)
- Black peppercorns (1 tablespoon)
- Red chili peppers (6-8, adjust to desired spiciness)
- Toor dal (2 tablespoons)
- Curry leaves (10-12)
- Asafoetida (a pinch)
- Turmeric powder (1/2 teaspoon)

Instructions:

1. Heat a dry pan over medium heat and add coriander seeds, cumin seeds, black peppercorns, and red chili peppers.

2. Toast the spices until fragrant, stirring occasionally. Be careful not to burn them.

3. Remove from heat and let the spices cool.

4. In the same pan, roast the toor dal until it turns golden brown and aromatic.

5. Add the curry leaves to the pan and roast for a few seconds until they become crisp.

6. Let the roasted spices and dal cool completely.

7. Transfer all the ingredients to a spice grinder or blender.

8. Add asafoetida and turmeric powder to the grinder.

9. Grind the ingredients into a fine powder.

10. Transfer the Rasam Powder to an airtight container for storage.

11. Store in a cool, dry place away from direct sunlight.

Rasam Powder is the key ingredient in preparing authentic rasam.

To make rasam, you can mix a spoonful of Rasam Powder with tamarind pulp, tomatoes, and various spices to create a tangy and aromatic broth.

This flavorful soup is often tempered with mustard seeds, curry leaves, and other seasonings.

Apart from using Rasam Powder for rasam, it can also be added to lentil soups, vegetable curries, and stews to enhance their flavors.

The combination of coriander seeds, cumin seeds, black peppercorns, and other spices in Rasam Powder provides a unique and delightful taste profile to your dishes.

Remember, homemade Rasam Powder offers the advantage of controlling the spice levels and adjusting the ingredients to suit your personal preferences.

You can experiment with the proportions of spices to create a blend that perfectly complements your taste buds.

Section 5: Vietnamese Pho and Spring Rolls:

Vietnamese cuisine is renowned for its fresh and vibrant flavors, and two iconic dishes that represent this cuisine are Pho and Spring Rolls.

Pho is a comforting noodle soup, while Spring Rolls are deliciously fresh and crispy rolls filled with a variety of ingredients.

Let's explore these dishes in more detail.

i. Pho:
Pho is a traditional Vietnamese soup made with a flavorful broth, rice noodles, and an assortment of toppings.

It is a staple dish in Vietnamese cuisine and is enjoyed throughout the country.

The broth for Pho is typically simmered for hours with a combination of aromatic herbs and spices, creating a rich and fragrant base.

Recipe: Pho

Ingredients:
- Beef bones or chicken bones (2-3 pounds)
- Onion (1 large, peeled and halved)
- Ginger (2-inch piece, sliced)
- Cinnamon stick (1)
- Star anise (2-3)
- Cloves (3-4)
- Cardamom pods (2-3)
- Beef or chicken broth (8 cups)
- Fish sauce (2 tablespoons)
- Sugar (1 tablespoon)
- Rice noodles (8-10 ounces, cooked according to package instructions)
- Sliced beef or chicken (optional)
- Bean sprouts, basil leaves, cilantro, lime wedges, and sliced chili peppers (for garnish)

Instructions:
1. In a large pot, add the beef or chicken bones, onion, and ginger. Toast them over medium heat until fragrant.

2. Add the cinnamon stick, star anise, cloves, and cardamom pods to the pot. Continue toasting for another minute.

3. Pour the beef or chicken broth into the pot.

Bring it to a boil, then reduce the heat to low and let it simmer for 1-2 hours, skimming off any impurities that rise to the surface.

4. After simmering, strain the broth to remove the bones and spices. Return the broth to the pot.

5. Season the broth with fish sauce and sugar, adjusting the amounts to taste.

6. If using sliced beef or chicken, blanch it in the broth until cooked to your liking.

7. To serve, divide the cooked rice noodles among bowls.

Ladle the hot broth over the noodles, along with the cooked meat if desired.

8. Garnish with bean sprouts, basil leaves, cilantro, lime wedges, and sliced chili peppers.

9. Serve Pho hot and enjoy!

ii. Spring Rolls:

Vietnamese Spring Rolls, also known as fresh or summer rolls, are a light and refreshing appetizer or snack.

They are made by wrapping a variety of fillings in rice paper wrappers.

The fillings often include vermicelli noodles, fresh herbs, vegetables, and protein such as shrimp, chicken, or tofu.

Recipe: Spring Rolls

Ingredients:
- Rice paper wrappers
- Rice vermicelli noodles (cooked according to package instructions)
- Shrimp (cooked and peeled), chicken (cooked and sliced), or tofu (sliced)
- Lettuce leaves (such as butter lettuce or romaine)
- Fresh herbs (mint leaves, Thai basil, cilantro)
- Carrot (julienned)

- Cucumber (julienned)
- Bean sprouts
- Hoisin sauce or peanut dipping sauce (for serving)

Instructions:
1. Fill a large bowl with warm water. Dip one rice paper wrapper into the water for a few seconds until it softens.

2. Place the softened rice paper wrapper on a clean, damp surface, such as a cutting board or plate.

3. Arrange a small portion of cooked rice vermicelli noodles in the middle of the wrapper.

4. Top the noodles with your choice of protein (such as shrimp, chicken, or tofu) followed by lettuce leaves, fresh herbs, julienned carrots, cucumber slices, and bean sprouts.

5. Fold the sides of the rice paper wrapper over the filling, then roll it tightly from the bottom to enclose the filling completely.

6. Repeat the process with the remaining ingredients to make more spring rolls.

7. Serve the spring rolls with a side of hoisin sauce or peanut dipping sauce for added flavor.

8. Enjoy the fresh and flavorful Vietnamese Spring Rolls!

Vietnamese Pho and Spring Rolls are beloved dishes that showcase the balance of flavors and textures in Vietnamese cuisine.

Whether you're savoring the aromatic broth of Pho or indulging in the crispiness of Spring Rolls, these dishes will transport your taste buds to the vibrant streets of Vietnam.

Chapter 5: African Flavors

Africa is a continent rich in diverse cultures and cuisines, each with its own unique flavors and ingredients.

In this chapter, we will embark on a culinary journey through the tantalizing tastes of Africa, exploring Moroccan Tagines and Couscous, Ethiopian Injera and Doro Wat, South African Braai and Bobotie, and Nigerian Jollof Rice and Suya.

In this chapter, we will learn about the traditional recipes, cooking techniques, and key ingredients that make African cuisine so special.

From the fragrant tagines of Morocco to the fiery flavors of Nigeria, each recipe will take us on a culinary adventure through the diverse and exciting flavors of Africa.

Get ready to experience the vibrant tastes and rich cultural heritage of African cuisine.

Section 1: Moroccan Tagines and Couscous

Moroccan cuisine is known for its aromatic spices, flavorful tagines, and fluffy couscous.

Tagines are slow-cooked stews typically prepared in a clay pot called a tagine, which helps infuse the flavors into the ingredients.

Couscous, a staple grain, is often served alongside tagines. Let's delve into the vibrant flavors of Moroccan cuisine.

i. Recipe: Moroccan Tagines and Couscous

Ingredients:
- 2 pounds of bone-in chicken or lamb, cut into pieces
- 2 tablespoons olive oil
- 1 onion, finely chopped
- 3 cloves of garlic, minced
- 2 teaspoons ground cumin
- 2 teaspoons ground coriander
- 1 teaspoon ground turmeric
- 1 teaspoon ground ginger
- 1 teaspoon paprika
- 1/2 teaspoon ground cinnamon
- 1/4 teaspoon cayenne pepper (optional, for heat)
- 1 cup diced tomatoes
- 2 cups chicken or vegetable broth
- 1 cup carrots, sliced
- 1 cup potatoes, cubed
- 1 cup zucchini, sliced
- 1 cup green olives (optional)
- Salt and pepper to taste
- Fresh cilantro or parsley for garnish

For the Couscous:
- 2 cups couscous
- 2 cups boiling water
- 1 tablespoon butter
- Salt to taste

Instructions:
1. Heat the olive oil in a large, heavy-bottomed pot or tagine over medium heat.

2. Add the chopped onion and minced garlic to the pot and sauté until they become translucent and fragrant.

3. Add the chicken or lamb pieces to the pot and brown them on all sides.

4. In a small bowl, mix together the cumin, coriander, turmeric, ginger, paprika, cinnamon, and cayenne pepper (if using).

Sprinkle this spice mixture over the meat and stir well to coat.

5. Add the diced tomatoes and broth to the pot, and season with salt and pepper to taste. Bring the mixture to a simmer.

6. Cover the pot and let the tagine simmer for about 1 hour, or until the meat is tender and cooked through. Stir occasionally and add more broth if needed.

7. While the tagine is simmering, prepare the couscous.

Place the couscous in a large bowl and pour boiling water over it.

Add butter and salt, then cover the bowl and let it sit for about 10 minutes, until the couscous absorbs the water and becomes fluffy.

Fluff it with a fork before serving.

8. In the last 15 minutes of cooking the tagine, add the carrots, potatoes, zucchini, and green olives (if using).

Continue cooking until the vegetables are tender.

9. Taste the tagine and adjust the seasoning if necessary.

10. Serve the Moroccan tagine hot over a bed of fluffy couscous.

Garnish with fresh cilantro or parsley for added freshness and aroma.

Enjoy the rich and aromatic flavors of Moroccan Tagines and Couscous, a dish that combines tender meat, flavorful spices, and hearty vegetables.

This traditional Moroccan recipe is sure to transport you to the vibrant streets of Marrakech with every bite.

Section 2: Ethiopian Injera and Doro Wat

Ethiopian cuisine offers a delightful combination of robust flavors and communal dining traditions.

Injera, a spongy fermented flatbread, serves as the foundation of Ethiopian meals.

Doro Wat, a spicy chicken stew, is a popular dish often enjoyed with injera.

Let's discover the unique and mouthwatering flavors of Ethiopian cuisine.

i. Recipe: Ethiopian Injera

Ingredients:
- 2 cups teff flour
- 3 cups water
- 1/4 teaspoon active dry yeast
- 1/2 teaspoon salt
- Vegetable oil for cooking

Instructions:
1. In a large bowl, combine the teff flour and water. Stir well until smooth and lump-free.

2. Cover the bowl with a clean kitchen towel and let it sit at room temperature for at least 24 hours.

This fermentation process helps develop the characteristic tangy flavor of injera.

3. After 24 hours, you will notice that the batter has risen and developed bubbles on the surface.

Give it a good stir.

4. Dissolve the yeast in a little water and add it to the batter. Stir well to incorporate.

5. Cover the bowl again and let it rest for another 1 to 2 hours to allow the yeast to activate and create a lighter texture.

6. Stir in the salt.

7. Heat a non-stick skillet or a large griddle over medium-high heat.

Lightly grease the surface with vegetable oil.

8. Pour about 1/4 cup of the batter onto the skillet and quickly swirl it around to spread it into a thin, circular shape.

The batter should sizzle as it hits the hot surface.

9. Cook the injera for about 2 to 3 minutes, or until the edges start to lift and the surface is covered in small holes.

Avoid flipping the injera as it is traditionally served with only one side cooked.

10. Remove the injera from the skillet and transfer it to a plate.

Repeat the process with the remaining batter, adding more oil to the skillet as needed.

11. Stack the injera on a plate, cover them with a clean kitchen towel to keep them warm and moist until serving.

Enjoy the unique and tangy flavor of Ethiopian Injera, a spongy and fermented flatbread that is perfect for scooping up savory stews and dishes.

ii. Recipe: Ethiopian Doro Wat

Ingredients:
- 1.5 pounds chicken pieces, skinless and bone-in
- 2 onions, finely chopped
- 4 cloves of garlic, minced
- 1-inch piece of ginger, grated
- 3 tablespoons Ethiopian berbere spice blend
- 2 tablespoons tomato paste
- 2 tablespoons oil
- 2 cups chicken broth
- Salt to taste
- Fresh cilantro for garnish (optional)

Instructions:
1. Heat the oil in a large, heavy-bottomed pot over medium heat.

2. Add the chopped onions to the pot and sauté until they become soft and golden brown.

3. Add the minced garlic and grated ginger to the pot and sauté for an additional minute until fragrant.

4. Stir in the berbere spice blend and tomato paste. Cook for a few minutes to allow the flavors to meld together.

5. Add the chicken pieces to the pot and coat them well with the spice mixture.

6. Pour in the chicken broth and season with salt to taste. Stir to combine.

7. Bring the mixture to a simmer, then reduce the heat to low and cover the pot.

 Let the Doro Wat cook slowly for about 1 to 1.5 hours, or until the chicken is tender and the flavors have melded together.

Stir occasionally and add more broth if needed.

8. Taste and adjust the seasoning if necessary.

9. Garnish the Doro Wat with fresh cilantro (optional).

10. Serve the Doro Wat hot with injera or steamed rice.

Indulge in the rich and spicy flavors of Ethiopian Doro Wat, a traditional chicken stew simmered in a fragrant blend of spices.

Pair it with the Ethiopian injera.

Section 3: South African Braai and Bobotie

South African cuisine is a melting pot of flavors influenced by various cultures and traditions.

The braai, a traditional South African barbecue, is a celebration of grilled meats and vibrant flavors.

Bobotie, a spiced minced meat dish topped with an egg-based custard, is a favorite comfort food in South Africa.

Join us as we explore the rich and diverse culinary heritage of South Africa.

i. Recipe: South African Braai

Ingredients:
- 2 pounds beef, lamb, or pork cuts (such as steaks, chops, or sausages)
- Salt and pepper to taste
- Marinade of your choice (such as a blend of olive oil, garlic, lemon juice, herbs, and spices)

Instructions:
1. Season the meat with salt and pepper on both sides.

2. Prepare your marinade by combining olive oil, minced garlic, lemon juice, herbs, and spices in a bowl.

3. Place the meat in a shallow dish or ziplock bag and pour the marinade over it.

Make sure the meat is coated evenly.

Cover the dish or seal the bag and let it marinate in the refrigerator for at least 1 hour, but preferably overnight for maximum flavor.

4. Preheat your grill or braai to medium-high heat.

5. Remove the meat from the marinade and discard any excess marinade.

6. Place the meat on the grill and cook to your desired doneness, flipping once halfway through.

Cooking times will vary depending on the type and thickness of the meat.

7. Once cooked, transfer the meat to a cutting board and let it rest for a few minutes.

8. Slice the meat against the grain and serve hot.

Enjoy the South African tradition of braai, a flavorful outdoor grilling experience that brings friends and family together.

ii. Recipe: South African Bobotie

Ingredients:
- 2 pounds ground beef
- 2 slices of bread, soaked in milk
- 1 onion, finely chopped
- 2 cloves of garlic, minced
- 2 tablespoons curry powder
- 1 tablespoon apricot jam or chutney
- 2 tablespoons vinegar
- 1 tablespoon Worcestershire sauce
- 1 tablespoon vegetable oil
- 1/2 cup raisins or sultanas
- 1/2 cup almonds, slivered or chopped
- 2 eggs
- 1 cup milk
- Salt and pepper to taste
- Bay leaves for garnish

Instructions:
1. Preheat your oven to 350°F (175°C).

2. Heat the vegetable oil in a large skillet or frying pan over medium heat.

3. Add the chopped onion and minced garlic to the pan and sauté until they become soft and translucent.

4. Add the ground beef to the pan and cook until browned, breaking it up into small pieces with a wooden spoon.

5. Stir in the curry powder, apricot jam or chutney, vinegar, Worcestershire sauce, raisins or sultanas, and almonds. Mix well to combine.

6. Remove the soaked bread from the milk and squeeze out any excess liquid.

Crumble the bread into the pan and stir it into the meat mixture.

7. Season with salt and pepper to taste.

Cook for a few more minutes to allow the flavors to meld together.

8. Transfer the meat mixture to a greased baking dish and spread it out evenly.

9. In a separate bowl, whisk together the eggs and milk.

Pour this mixture over the meat in the baking dish.

10. Place a few bay leaves on top for garnish.

11. Bake the Bobotie in the preheated oven for about 40 to 45 minutes, or until the custard topping is set and golden brown.

12. Remove from the oven and let it cool for a few minutes before serving.

Delight in the flavors of South African Bobotie, a savory and spiced minced meat dish with a custard topping that is perfect for a hearty meal.

Serve it with rice and chutney for a complete culinary experience.

Section 4: Nigerian Jollof Rice and Suya

Nigerian cuisine is known for its bold and vibrant flavors.

Jollof Rice, a one-pot rice dish cooked with tomatoes, onions, and an array of spices, is a beloved and iconic Nigerian dish.

Suya, a popular street food, features skewered and grilled meat seasoned with a spicy peanut-based marinade.

Let's savor the aromatic and spicy flavors of Nigerian cuisine.

i. Recipe: Nigerian Jollof Rice

Ingredients:
- 2 cups long-grain parboiled rice
- 1 onion, finely chopped
- 2-3 ripe tomatoes, blended into a puree
- 1 red bell pepper, blended into a puree
- 1 green bell pepper, finely chopped
- 2 cloves of garlic, minced
- 1 teaspoon thyme
- 1 teaspoon curry powder
- 1 teaspoon paprika
- 1/2 teaspoon cayenne pepper (optional, for heat)
- 2 cups chicken or vegetable broth
- 1 cup cooked or canned red kidney beans (optional)

- 2 tablespoons vegetable oil
- Salt to taste

Instructions:
1. Rinse the parboiled rice with cold water until the water runs clear. Drain and set aside.

2. Heat the vegetable oil in a large pot over medium heat.

3. Add the chopped onion and minced garlic to the pot and sauté until they become soft and fragrant.

4. Add the tomato puree and bell pepper puree to the pot and stir well to combine.

Cook for about 5 minutes to reduce the moisture and concentrate the flavors.

5. Stir in the thyme, curry powder, paprika, and cayenne pepper (if using).

Mix well.

6. Add the drained rice to the pot and stir to coat it with the tomato and pepper mixture.

7. Pour in the chicken or vegetable broth and bring the mixture to a boil.

8. Reduce the heat to low, cover the pot with a tight-fitting lid, and let the rice simmer for about 20-25 minutes, or until the rice is tender and cooked through.

9. If using, add the cooked or canned red kidney beans to the pot and stir gently to incorporate them into the rice.

10. Season with salt to taste and adjust the seasonings if desired.

11. Remove the pot from the heat and let it sit, covered, for a few minutes before fluffing the rice with a fork.

12. Serve the Nigerian Jollof Rice hot as a main dish or as a side dish to complement other Nigerian delicacies.

Enjoy the rich and flavorful Nigerian Jollof Rice, a beloved West African dish known for its vibrant color and tantalizing taste.

ii. Recipe: Nigerian Suya

Ingredients:
- 1 pound beef or chicken, thinly sliced
- 1/4 cup peanut butter
- 2 tablespoons ground roasted peanuts
- 2 tablespoons vegetable oil
- 1 tablespoon paprika
- 1 tablespoon garlic powder
- 1 tablespoon onion powder
- 1 teaspoon cayenne pepper (adjust according to heat preference)
- 1 teaspoon dried thyme
- 1 teaspoon ground ginger
- 1 teaspoon ground nutmeg
- Salt to taste
- Skewers for grilling

Instructions:
1. In a bowl, combine the peanut butter, ground roasted peanuts, vegetable oil, paprika, garlic powder, onion powder, cayenne pepper, dried thyme, ground ginger, ground nutmeg, and salt.

Mix well to form a thick paste.

2. Add the sliced beef or chicken to the bowl and toss to coat the meat evenly with the spice paste.

Let it marinate in the refrigerator for at least 1 hour, but preferably overnight for the flavors to develop.

3. If using wooden skewers, soak them in water for about 30 minutes to prevent them from burning during grilling.

4. Preheat your grill or barbecue to medium-high heat.

5. Thread the marinated meat onto the skewers, ensuring an even distribution.

6. Place the skewers on the preheated grill and cook for about 8-10 minutes or until the meat is cooked to your desired doneness, turning the skewers occasionally to ensure even grilling.

7. While grilling, you can brush the meat with any remaining marinade for added flavor and moisture.

8. Once the meat is cooked, remove the skewers from the grill and let them rest for a few minutes.

9. Serve the Nigerian Suya hot, garnished with additional ground roasted peanuts and accompanied by sliced onions and fresh tomatoes for a traditional touch.

10. Enjoy the delicious and spicy Nigerian Suya, a popular street food known for its smoky, tangy, and nutty flavors.

Note: Nigerian Suya can also be enjoyed with a side of spicy peanut sauce or served with grilled vegetables and flatbread for a complete meal.

Indulge in the vibrant and diverse flavors of Nigerian cuisine with the aromatic Jollof Rice and the tantalizing Suya, capturing the essence of West African culinary delights.

Enjoy.

Chapter 6: Latin American Delights

Introduction to Latin American Cuisine

Latin American cuisine is a vibrant fusion of flavors, colors, and cultural influences.

From the sizzling street food of Mexico to the mouthwatering grills of Argentina, and the rich stews of Brazil, this chapter explores the diverse and delicious culinary traditions of Latin America.

Get ready to embark on a culinary journey through this region known for its bold and flavorful dishes.

Section 1: Mexican Tacos and Guacamole

Mexican cuisine is renowned for its vibrant spices and bold flavors.

In this section, we delve into the world of Mexican tacos and guacamole, two iconic dishes that have captured the hearts and palates of food lovers worldwide.

- Introduction to Mexican Cuisine

Mexican cuisine is a celebration of fresh ingredients, bold spices, and complex flavors.

From street vendors to fine dining establishments, Mexican food offers a diverse range of dishes that showcase the country's rich culinary heritage.

i. - Tacos

Tacos are a beloved Mexican street food, featuring a variety of fillings, salsas, and toppings.

Whether it's the classic carne asada, tender carnitas, or flavorful grilled vegetables, tacos are a versatile and satisfying meal.

 Learn how to make authentic corn tortillas and explore a variety of tantalizing taco fillings.

Recipe: Tacos

Ingredients:
- 1 pound ground beef or your choice of protein (such as chicken, pork, or tofu)
- 1 tablespoon oil
- 1 small onion, finely diced
- 2 cloves garlic, minced
- 1 tablespoon chili powder
- 1 teaspoon ground cumin
- 1/2 teaspoon paprika
- 1/2 teaspoon dried oregano
- Salt and pepper to taste
- Taco shells or tortillas
- Toppings of your choice (such as shredded lettuce, diced tomatoes, grated cheese, sour cream, salsa, guacamole)

Instructions:
1. Heat the oil in a large skillet over medium heat. Add the diced onion and minced garlic, and cook until softened and fragrant, about 2-3 minutes.

2. Add the ground beef (or your choice of protein) to the skillet and cook, breaking it up with a spoon, until browned and cooked through.

3. Stir in the chili powder, ground cumin, paprika, dried oregano, salt, and pepper.

Cook for an additional 2-3 minutes to allow the flavors to meld together.

4. Warm the taco shells or tortillas according to the package instructions.

5. Assemble the tacos by filling each shell or tortilla with the cooked meat mixture.

Top with your choice of toppings, such as shredded lettuce, diced tomatoes, grated cheese, sour cream, salsa, and guacamole.

6. Serve the tacos immediately and enjoy!

Note: Feel free to customize your tacos with additional toppings and condiments according to your preference.

You can also add a squeeze of lime juice or sprinkle some chopped cilantro for added freshness and flavor.

ii. Guacamole

No Mexican meal is complete without a bowl of creamy and flavorful guacamole.

Made with ripe avocados, fresh lime juice, cilantro, and other seasonings, guacamole is a versatile dip that can be enjoyed with tortilla chips or used as a condiment for tacos, burritos, and other Mexican dishes.

Discover the secrets to making the perfect guacamole that will impress your family and friends.

Recipe: Guacamole

Ingredients:
- 2 ripe avocados
- 1 small onion, finely diced
- 1 small tomato, diced
- 1 jalapeno pepper, seeded and minced (optional)
- 1 clove garlic, minced
- Juice of 1 lime
- 1/4 cup fresh cilantro, chopped
- Salt and pepper to taste

Instructions:
1. Cut the avocados in half, remove the pits, and scoop out the flesh into a bowl.

2. Mash the avocados with a fork until desired consistency is reached (smooth or slightly chunky).

3. Add the diced onion, diced tomato, minced jalapeno pepper (if using), minced garlic, lime juice, and chopped cilantro to the bowl with the mashed avocados.

4. Stir everything together until well combined.

5. Season with salt and pepper to taste.

Adjust the amount of lime juice and jalapeno pepper based on your preference for acidity and spiciness.

6. Transfer the guacamole to a serving bowl and cover with plastic wrap, ensuring the wrap is pressed directly against the surface of the guacamole to prevent browning.

7. Let the guacamole sit at room temperature for about 30 minutes to allow the flavors to meld together.

8. Serve the guacamole with tortilla chips, as a topping for tacos or burritos, or as a dip for vegetables.

Note: Guacamole is best enjoyed fresh but can be refrigerated for up to 24 hours.

To prevent browning, place a piece of plastic wrap directly on the surface of the guacamole and store it in an airtight container in the refrigerator.

Before serving, give it a stir and adjust the seasoning if needed.

Section 2: Argentinian Asado and Empanadas

Argentina is known for its love of meat and grilling, and the asado, a traditional Argentine barbecue, is a culinary experience like no other.

Alongside the asado, empanadas, savory stuffed pastries, are a popular snack enjoyed throughout the country.

- Introduction to Argentinian Cuisine

Argentinian cuisine is heavily influenced by European immigrants, particularly from Italy and Spain.

The country's cuisine is characterized by its high-quality beef, hearty stews, and delectable pastries.

Dive into the flavors of Argentina and learn about its culinary traditions.

- Asado

The asado is a cherished culinary tradition in Argentina, where friends and families gather around the grill to enjoy an array of succulent grilled meats.

Discover the art of preparing and grilling various cuts of meat, from juicy beef steaks to flavorful sausages, and learn about the cultural significance of the asado in Argentinian society.

i. Recipe: Asado

Ingredients:
- 2 pounds beef ribs or your choice of beef cuts (such as flank steak, short ribs, or ribeye)
- Salt and pepper to taste
- Chimichurri sauce (for serving, optional)

Instructions:
1. Preheat a grill or barbecue to medium-high heat.

2. Season the beef ribs or cuts with salt and pepper, ensuring both sides are evenly coated.

3. Place the beef on the grill and cook for about 5-7 minutes per side, or until desired doneness is reached.

Adjust the cooking time based on the thickness of the meat and your preference for doneness.

4. While grilling, you can occasionally brush the meat with some chimichurri sauce for added flavor, if desired.

Alternatively, reserve the chimichurri sauce for serving as a condiment.

5. Once cooked to your liking, remove the beef from the grill and let it rest for a few minutes.

6. Slice the beef into individual portions or serve it as whole cuts.

7. Serve the asado with chimichurri sauce on the side for dipping or drizzling, if desired.

8. Enjoy the flavorful and tender grilled beef asado!

Note: Asado is a popular Argentine barbecue tradition that involves slow-cooking and grilling various cuts of meat.

Feel free to experiment with different cuts of beef and adjust the seasoning to suit your taste preferences.

Serve the asado with traditional accompaniments like chimichurri sauce, grilled vegetables, and a side of crusty bread.

- Empanadas

Empanadas are a staple in Argentinian cuisine, featuring a savory filling encased in a buttery pastry crust.

These handheld delights come in various flavors, including beef, chicken, cheese, and vegetable fillings.

Master the art of making empanadas from scratch and explore different filling options to create your own flavor combinations.

ii. Recipe: Empanadas

Ingredients:
For the dough:

- 2 1/2 cups all-purpose flour
- 1/2 teaspoon salt
- 1/2 cup unsalted butter, cold and cubed
- 1/2 cup water, cold

For the filling:
- 1 tablespoon olive oil
- 1 small onion, finely chopped
- 1 bell pepper, finely chopped
- 1 pound ground beef or your choice of filling (chicken, cheese, or vegetables)
- 2 cloves garlic, minced
- 1 teaspoon ground cumin
- 1 teaspoon paprika
- Salt and pepper to taste
- 1/4 cup chopped green olives (optional)
- 1/4 cup raisins (optional)
- 1 egg, beaten (for egg wash)

Instructions:
1. In a large bowl, whisk together the flour and salt for the dough.

Add the cold cubed butter and use a pastry cutter or your fingers to cut the butter into the flour until it resembles coarse crumbs.

2. Gradually add the cold water, a little at a time, and mix until the dough comes together.

Shape the dough into a ball, wrap it in plastic wrap, and refrigerate for at least 30 minutes.

3. In a skillet, heat the olive oil over medium heat.

Add the chopped onion and bell pepper and sauté until they become tender and slightly caramelized.

4. Add the ground beef (or your choice of filling) to the skillet and cook until it is browned.

Break up the meat with a spatula as it cooks.

5. Stir in the minced garlic, ground cumin, paprika, salt, and pepper.

Cook for an additional 2-3 minutes to allow the flavors to meld together.

6. If using, add the chopped green olives and raisins to the skillet and mix well.

Remove the skillet from the heat and let the filling cool.

7. Preheat the oven to 375°F (190°C) and line a baking sheet with parchment paper.

8. On a lightly floured surface, roll out the chilled dough to a thickness of about 1/8 inch.

Use a round cookie cutter or a glass to cut out circles of about 4-6 inches in diameter.

9. Spoon a portion of the filling onto the center of each dough circle.

Fold the dough over the filling to create a half-moon shape.

Press the edges firmly to seal the empanadas.

You can also use a fork to crimp the edges.

10. Place the filled empanadas on the prepared baking sheet.

Brush the tops with beaten egg to give them a golden color when baked.

11. Bake the empanadas for 20-25 minutes, or until they are golden brown and crisp.

12. Remove from the oven and let them cool for a few minutes before serving.

Empanadas can be served warm or at room temperature.

Note: Empanadas are versatile and can be filled with various ingredients.

Feel free to experiment with different fillings such as cheese, vegetables, or even sweet fillings like fruit or chocolate.

Serve the empanadas as a snack, appetizer, or main dish, and accompany them with your favorite dipping sauces or salsa.

Section 3: Brazilian Feijoada and Brigadeiros

Brazilian cuisine is a reflection of the country's diverse cultural heritage, combining indigenous, African, and Portuguese influences.

In this section, we explore two iconic Brazilian dishes: feijoada, a hearty black bean stew, and brigadeiros, sweet chocolate truffles.

- Introduction to Brazilian Cuisine

Brazilian cuisine is a melting pot of flavors, with regional variations and a wide array of tropical ingredients.

From the Amazon rainforest to the coastal regions, Brazilian cuisine offers a diverse range of dishes that showcase the country's culinary richness.

- Feijoada

Feijoada is considered the national dish of Brazil, a hearty black bean stew that is typically made with a variety of pork cuts, such as sausage, bacon, and ribs.

This flavorful and comforting dish is traditionally served with rice, collard greens, and farofa (toasted cassava flour).

Discover the techniques and ingredients needed to create an authentic Brazilian feijoada that will transport your taste buds to the vibrant streets of Brazil.

i. Recipe: Feijoada

Ingredients:
- 1 pound black beans, dried
- 1 pound assorted pork meats (such as pork shoulder, ribs, and sausage)
- 1 onion, chopped
- 4 cloves garlic, minced
- 2 bay leaves
- 4 tablespoons vegetable oil
- 1 tablespoon smoked paprika
- 1 teaspoon ground cumin
- Salt and pepper to taste
- 2 oranges, sliced (for serving)
- 1 bunch fresh parsley, chopped (for garnish)
- Rice, farofa (toasted cassava flour), and collard greens (for serving)

Instructions:
1. Rinse the black beans and place them in a large bowl.

Cover with water and let them soak overnight.

Drain and set aside.

2. In a large pot, add the soaked beans, pork meats, chopped onion, minced garlic, and bay leaves.

Cover with water and bring to a boil over high heat.

3. Reduce the heat to low and let the beans and meats simmer for about 2 hours, or until the beans are tender and the meats are cooked through.

4. While the beans and meats are cooking, heat the vegetable oil in a skillet over medium heat.

Add the smoked paprika and ground cumin, and cook for a minute to release their flavors.

5. Remove a cup of the cooked beans from the pot and mash them with a fork.

Return the mashed beans to the pot and stir well to thicken the broth.

6. Add the seasoned oil mixture to the pot and stir to incorporate it into the beans and meats.

Simmer for another 30 minutes to allow the flavors to meld together.

Season with salt and pepper to taste.

7. Remove the bay leaves from the pot and discard.

8. Serve the feijoada hot, accompanied by cooked rice, farofa, collard greens, and orange slices.

Garnish with chopped parsley.

9. Traditionally, feijoada is enjoyed by spooning a portion of beans, meats, and rice onto the plate, and then adding farofa and collard greens on the side.

The orange slices can be squeezed over the feijoada to add a fresh citrus flavor.

Note: Feijoada is a hearty and flavorful Brazilian dish that is typically enjoyed as a main course.

It is often served during special occasions and gatherings.

The combination of black beans and various pork meats creates a rich and satisfying flavor.

Feel free to customize the meats used in the recipe based on your preference and availability.

Leftover feijoada can be stored in the refrigerator and reheated for future meals.

- Brigadeiros

Brigadeiros are Brazil's beloved sweet treat, often enjoyed at parties and celebrations.

These fudgy chocolate truffles are made from condensed milk, cocoa powder, butter, and chocolate sprinkles.

Learn how to make brigadeiros from scratch and explore variations like coconut, peanut, or even brigadeiro cake.

These bite-sized delights are sure to satisfy any sweet tooth.

ii. Recipe: Brigadeiros

Ingredients:
- 1 can (14 ounces) sweetened condensed milk
- 2 tablespoons unsweetened cocoa powder
- 2 tablespoons unsalted butter
- Chocolate sprinkles, for coating

Instructions:
1. In a medium saucepan, combine the sweetened condensed milk, cocoa powder, and butter.

2. Place the saucepan over medium heat and stir constantly with a wooden spoon to prevent the mixture from burning.

3. Continue stirring until the mixture thickens and starts to pull away from the sides of the saucepan, forming a thick, fudgy consistency.

This should take about 10-15 minutes.

4. Remove the saucepan from the heat and let the mixture cool slightly until it is safe to handle.

5. Grease your hands with a little butter or oil to prevent sticking.

Take small portions of the mixture and roll them into small, bite-sized balls, about 1 inch in diameter.

6. Place the chocolate sprinkles in a shallow bowl.

Roll each brigadeiro ball in the sprinkles, coating them evenly.

7. Transfer the brigadeiros to a parchment-lined plate or baking sheet.

Repeat the process until all the mixture is used.

8. Place the plate of brigadeiros in the refrigerator for about 30 minutes to allow them to firm up.

9. Once chilled, the brigadeiros are ready to be enjoyed.

Serve them at room temperature.

10. Store any leftovers in an airtight container in the refrigerator for up to 5 days.

Note: Brigadeiros are a popular Brazilian sweet treat, often served at parties and celebrations. They have a rich, chocolatey flavor and a fudgy texture.

Feel free to get creative with the coatings and toppings for brigadeiros.

In addition to chocolate sprinkles, you can use other toppings like shredded coconut, crushed nuts, or colored sugar.

Enjoy these delightful confections as a snack or as a sweet ending to a meal.

Section 4: Peruvian Ceviche and Lomo Saltado

Peruvian cuisine has gained international recognition for its unique flavors and diverse culinary traditions.

In this section, we delve into two iconic Peruvian dishes: ceviche, a refreshing seafood dish, and lomo saltado, a flavorful stir-fry that combines Peruvian and Chinese influences.

- Introduction to Peruvian Cuisine

Peruvian cuisine is a fusion of indigenous ingredients, Spanish influence, and Asian flavors brought by immigrants.

It's known for its use of fresh seafood, vibrant spices, and unique ingredients like aji amarillo (yellow chili pepper) and quinoa.

Explore the fascinating flavors and cultural influences that shape Peruvian cuisine.

- Ceviche

Ceviche is a refreshing and tangy dish made with raw fish or seafood marinated in citrus juices, such as lime or lemon, and seasoned with onions, cilantro, and chili peppers.

Discover the art of preparing ceviche, including the different variations like traditional fish ceviche, mixed seafood ceviche, or even vegetarian options.

Experience the burst of flavors and textures that make Peruvian ceviche a true culinary delight.

i. Recipe: Ceviche

Ingredients:
- 1 pound white fish fillets (such as snapper, tilapia, or sea bass), cut into small cubes
- 1 cup freshly squeezed lime juice
- 1 red onion, thinly sliced
- 1 jalapeno pepper, seeded and finely chopped
- 1 red bell pepper, diced
- 1/2 cup chopped fresh cilantro
- 2 tomatoes, diced
- Salt and pepper to taste
- Tortilla chips or lettuce leaves, for serving

Instructions:

1. In a glass or ceramic bowl, place the fish cubes and pour the lime juice over them.

Make sure the fish is fully submerged in the lime juice.

Let it marinate in the refrigerator for about 30 minutes to 1 hour.

The lime juice will "cook" the fish and give it a tender texture.

2. After marinating, drain the lime juice from the fish and discard it.

3. Add the sliced red onion, jalapeno pepper, red bell pepper, chopped cilantro, and diced tomatoes to the bowl with the fish.

4. Season with salt and pepper to taste.

Gently toss all the ingredients together until well combined.

5. Cover the bowl and refrigerate for at least 1 hour to allow the flavors to meld together.

6. Before serving, give the ceviche a quick stir.

Taste and adjust the seasoning if needed.

7. Serve the ceviche chilled, either on its own as a refreshing appetizer or with tortilla chips for scooping.

Alternatively, you can serve it wrapped in lettuce leaves for a lighter option.

Note: Ceviche is a popular Latin American dish, particularly in coastal regions.

It is made by marinating raw fish or seafood in citrus juice, which effectively "cooks" the fish through the acid.

The result is a light and flavorful dish with a tangy citrus taste.

Feel free to customize your ceviche by adding other ingredients like avocado, cucumber, or mango.

Enjoy this refreshing and zesty dish as a starter or as part of a summer meal.

- Lomo Saltado

Lomo saltado is a popular Peruvian stir-fry that combines marinated strips of beef, onions, tomatoes, and spices.

This flavorful dish is often served with fries and rice, showcasing the fusion of Peruvian and Chinese flavors.

Learn the techniques to achieve the perfect balance of tender beef, crisp vegetables, and bold seasonings in this beloved Peruvian comfort food.

ii. Recipe: Lomo Saltado

Ingredients:
- 1 pound beef tenderloin, thinly sliced
- 2 tablespoons vegetable oil
- 1 red onion, thinly sliced
- 1 red bell pepper, cut into strips
- 2 tomatoes, cut into wedges
- 3 cloves garlic, minced
- 2 tablespoons soy sauce

- 2 tablespoons vinegar (preferably red wine vinegar)
- 1 teaspoon ground cumin
- Salt and pepper to taste
- Fresh cilantro leaves, for garnish
- Cooked white rice, for serving
- French fries, for serving

Instructions:
1. In a large skillet or wok, heat the vegetable oil over high heat.

2. Add the beef slices to the skillet and cook until browned on all sides.

Remove the beef from the skillet and set aside.

3. In the same skillet, add the sliced red onion and red bell pepper.

Stir-fry for a few minutes until the vegetables are slightly softened.

4. Add the minced garlic to the skillet and cook for another minute.

5. Return the cooked beef to the skillet with the vegetables.
6. In a small bowl, whisk together the soy sauce, vinegar, and ground cumin.

Pour the sauce over the beef and vegetables in the skillet.

7. Season with salt and pepper to taste. Stir everything together to coat the beef and vegetables evenly with the sauce.

8. Continue cooking for a few more minutes until the beef is cooked to your desired doneness and the vegetables are crisp-tender.

9. Remove the skillet from heat and garnish with fresh cilantro leaves.

10. Serve the lomo saltado hot over cooked white rice and accompanied by French fries on the side.

The combination of tender beef, sautéed vegetables, and flavorful sauce makes for a delicious and satisfying meal.

Note: Lomo saltado is a popular Peruvian dish that combines Chinese and Peruvian flavors.

It features marinated beef stir-fried with onions, tomatoes, and peppers, seasoned with soy sauce and spices.

The dish is typically served over white rice and accompanied by French fries, adding a unique touch to its presentation.

Lomo saltado is known for its bold and savory flavors, making it a favorite among both meat lovers and fans of Peruvian cuisine.

Enjoy this hearty and delicious dish that showcases the fusion of cultures in Peruvian cuisine.

Conclusion

Latin American cuisine is a celebration of vibrant flavors, cultural diversity, and culinary traditions that have been passed down through generations.

From the spicy tacos of Mexico to the sizzling grills of Argentina and the exotic flavors of Brazil and Peru, this chapter has explored the rich tapestry of Latin American delights.

Embark on your own culinary journey and bring the vibrant tastes of Latin America into your kitchen.

Chapter 7: Middle Eastern Cuisine

Introduction to Middle Eastern Cuisine

Middle Eastern cuisine is a rich and diverse culinary tradition that encompasses a wide range of flavors, ingredients, and cooking techniques.

This chapter explores the vibrant and aromatic dishes from Lebanon, Turkey, Israel, and Iran, offering a glimpse into the delicious world of Middle Eastern gastronomy.

From appetizing mezze platters to succulent kebabs and mouthwatering desserts, prepare to embark on a culinary journey through the flavors of the Middle East.

Section 1: Lebanese Mezze and Shawarma

Lebanese cuisine is renowned for its mezze, a selection of small dishes served as appetizers or a meal in themselves.

These dishes are often packed with bold flavors and vibrant ingredients.

Additionally, the chapter explores the popular Lebanese street food, shawarma, featuring tender meat roasted on a vertical spit and served in warm pita bread with flavorful sauces and garnishes.

Lebanese Mezze dishes include: baba ganoush, tabbouleh, falafel, and hummus

i. Recipe: Baba Ganoush

Ingredients:
- 2 large eggplants

- 3 tablespoons tahini
- 3 tablespoons lemon juice
- 2 garlic cloves, minced
- 2 tablespoons olive oil
- Salt, to taste
- Paprika, for garnish
- Fresh parsley, for garnish

Instructions:
1. Preheat the oven to 400°F (200°C).

Place the eggplants on a baking sheet and pierce them with a fork several times.

2. Roast the eggplants in the oven for 40-45 minutes, or until they become soft and collapse.

3. Remove the eggplants from the oven and let them cool.

Once cooled, peel off the skin and discard.

4. Place the cooked eggplant flesh in a bowl and mash it with a fork until smooth.

5. Add the tahini, lemon juice, minced garlic, olive oil, and salt. Mix well to combine all the ingredients.

6. Transfer the baba ganoush to a serving dish. Drizzle with olive oil and sprinkle with paprika.

7. Garnish with fresh parsley.

8. Serve with warm pita bread or vegetable sticks.

ii. Recipe: Tabbouleh

Ingredients:

- 1 cup bulgur wheat
- 2 cups chopped fresh parsley
- 1/2 cup chopped fresh mint
- 1/2 cup diced tomatoes
- 1/2 cup diced cucumbers
- 1/4 cup finely chopped red onion
- 3 tablespoons lemon juice
- 3 tablespoons olive oil
- Salt and pepper, to taste

Instructions:
1. Place the bulgur wheat in a bowl and cover it with boiling water.

Let it sit for about 20 minutes, or until the wheat is tender.

2. Drain any excess water from the bulgur wheat and fluff it with a fork.

3. In a large mixing bowl, combine the cooked bulgur wheat, chopped parsley, chopped mint, diced tomatoes, diced cucumbers, and finely chopped red onion.

4. In a separate small bowl, whisk together the lemon juice, olive oil, salt, and pepper.

5. Pour the dressing over the tabbouleh salad and toss to combine all the ingredients.

6. Adjust the seasoning with salt and pepper, if needed.

7. Let the tabbouleh salad sit for at least 30 minutes to allow the flavors to meld together.

8. Serve chilled or at room temperature as part of your mezze spread.

iii. Recipe: Falafel

Ingredients:
- 1 cup dried chickpeas
- 1 small onion, roughly chopped
- 4 garlic cloves
- 1 cup fresh parsley leaves
- 1 teaspoon ground cumin
- 1 teaspoon ground coriander
- 1/2 teaspoon baking soda
- Salt, to taste
- Vegetable oil, for frying

Instructions:
1. Place the dried chickpeas in a bowl and cover them with water.

Let them soak overnight. Drain and rinse before using.

2. In a food processor, combine the soaked chickpeas, onion, garlic cloves, fresh parsley, ground cumin, ground coriander, baking soda, and a pinch of salt.

3. Pulse the mixture until well combined and forms a coarse paste.

Be careful not to over-process.

4. Transfer the falafel mixture to a bowl and refrigerate for at least 1 hour to firm up.

5. Heat vegetable oil in a deep pot or frying pan to 350°F (175°C).

6. Shape the falafel mixture into small balls or patties, about 1 inch in diameter.

7. Fry the falafel in batches until golden brown and crispy, about 3-4 minutes per batch.

Make sure to flip them halfway through for even cooking.

8. Remove the falafel from the oil using a slotted spoon and place them on a plate lined with paper towels to absorb any excess oil.

9. Serve the falafel hot as part of your mezze spread.

They can be enjoyed on their own, stuffed in pita bread with tahini sauce, or served alongside other mezze dishes.

Note: You can also bake the falafel for a healthier alternative.

Preheat the oven to 375°F (190°C).

Place the falafel on a baking sheet lined with parchment paper and lightly brush them with olive oil.

Bake for 20-25 minutes, flipping halfway through, until they are golden brown and crispy.

Enjoy these delicious mezze dishes as part of your Lebanese spread!

iv. Recipe: Hummus

Ingredients:
- 1 can of chickpeas, drained and rinsed
- 3 tablespoons tahini
- 3 tablespoons lemon juice
- 2 garlic cloves, minced
- 2 tablespoons olive oil
- 1/2 teaspoon ground cumin
- Salt, to taste
- Paprika, for garnish
- Fresh parsley, for garnish

Instructions:
1. In a food processor, combine the chickpeas, tahini, lemon juice, garlic, olive oil, cumin, and a pinch of salt.

2. Blend until smooth and creamy.

If needed, add a little water to achieve the desired consistency.

3. Taste and adjust the seasoning with salt if necessary.

4. Transfer the hummus to a serving dish.

Drizzle with olive oil and sprinkle with paprika.

5. Garnish with fresh parsley.

6. Serve with warm pita bread or fresh vegetables for dipping.

Enjoy the creamy and flavorful hummus as part of your Lebanese mezze spread.

It pairs well with other mezze dishes like baba ganoush, tabbouleh, and falafe above.

v. Recipe: Lebanese Shawarma

Ingredients:
- 1.5 pounds boneless skinless chicken thighs or beef strips
- 1/4 cup olive oil
- 4 cloves garlic, minced
- 2 tablespoons lemon juice
- 2 tablespoons plain yogurt
- 1 tablespoon ground cumin
- 1 tablespoon ground coriander
- 1 teaspoon paprika

- 1 teaspoon ground turmeric
- 1/2 teaspoon ground cinnamon
- 1/2 teaspoon ground cardamom
- 1/2 teaspoon salt
- 1/4 teaspoon black pepper
- Pita bread or flatbread, for serving
- Toppings and sauces of your choice (such as tahini sauce, garlic sauce, pickles, tomatoes, and lettuce)

Instructions:
1. In a bowl, combine olive oil, minced garlic, lemon juice, plain yogurt, ground cumin, ground coriander, paprika, ground turmeric, ground cinnamon, ground cardamom, salt, and black pepper.

Mix well to form a marinade.

2. Place the chicken thighs or beef strips in the marinade and coat them evenly.

Cover the bowl and refrigerate for at least 2 hours or overnight for the flavors to develop.

3. Preheat the grill or a stovetop griddle pan over medium-high heat.

4. Remove the marinated chicken thighs or beef strips from the refrigerator and let them sit at room temperature for about 10 minutes.

5. If using a grill, grill the marinated meat for about 6-8 minutes per side, or until fully cooked and slightly charred.

If using a griddle pan, cook the meat for the same amount of time, flipping halfway through.

6. Once cooked, transfer the meat to a cutting board and let it rest for a few minutes.

7. Slice the grilled chicken or beef into thin strips or bite-sized pieces.

8. Warm the pita bread or flatbread on the grill or in a pan for a few seconds on each side.

9. Assemble the shawarma by placing the sliced meat onto the warmed pita bread or flatbread.

Add your desired toppings and sauces, such as tahini sauce, garlic sauce, pickles, tomatoes, and lettuce.

10. Roll the bread tightly around the filling, securing it with foil or parchment paper if needed.

11. Serve the Lebanese shawarma warm and enjoy the flavorful combination of tender meat and delicious toppings.

Savor the authentic taste of Lebanese shawarma, a popular street food known for its tantalizing blend of spices and textures!

Section 2: Turkish Kebabs and Baklava

Turkish cuisine is celebrated for its succulent kebabs and rich desserts.

Discover the art of grilling perfectly seasoned kebabs, whether it's juicy lamb, marinated chicken, or flavorful vegetarian options.

The chapter also delves into the world of baklava, a sweet pastry made of layers of filo dough filled with nuts and drenched in a fragrant syrup, showcasing the delightful combination of crunchy and sweet flavors.

i. Recipe: Turkish Kebabs

Ingredients:
- 1 lb (450g) boneless meat (beef, lamb, or chicken), cut into cubes
- 1 onion, finely chopped
- 2 cloves of garlic, minced
- 2 tablespoons olive oil
- 1 tablespoon lemon juice
- 1 teaspoon ground cumin
- 1 teaspoon ground paprika
- 1 teaspoon ground coriander
- Salt and pepper to taste
- Skewers, soaked in water if using wooden skewers

Instructions:
1. In a bowl, combine the chopped onion, minced garlic, olive oil, lemon juice, ground cumin, ground paprika, ground coriander, salt, and pepper.

Mix well to create a marinade.

2. Add the cubed meat to the marinade and toss to coat evenly.

Cover the bowl with plastic wrap or transfer the mixture to a resealable bag.

Allow the meat to marinate in the refrigerator for at least 1 hour, or overnight for best flavor.

3. Preheat your grill or grill pan to medium-high heat.

4. Thread the marinated meat onto the skewers, alternating with pieces of onion or bell pepper if desired.

5. Place the kebabs on the preheated grill and cook for about 8-10 minutes, turning occasionally, until the meat is cooked through and nicely charred on the outside.

6. Remove the kebabs from the grill and let them rest for a few minutes before serving.

7. Serve the Turkish kebabs hot with pita bread, rice, or a side salad.

They can be enjoyed with yogurt sauce, tzatziki, or a squeeze of lemon juice.

Note: If you prefer, you can also cook the kebabs in the oven.

Preheat the oven to 400°F (200°C) and place the skewers on a baking sheet lined with parchment paper.

Bake for about 15-20 minutes or until the meat is cooked through.

Enjoy these flavorful Turkish kebabs as part of your Middle Eastern culinary journey!

Recipe: Baklava

Ingredients:
- 1 package of phyllo dough (about 16 oz or 450g)
- 1 cup unsalted butter, melted
- 2 cups finely chopped nuts (such as walnuts, pistachios, or almonds)
- 1 cup granulated sugar
- 1 teaspoon ground cinnamon
- 1/2 teaspoon ground cloves
- 1/2 cup honey
- 1/4 cup water

- 1 teaspoon lemon juice

Instructions:
1. Preheat your oven to 350°F (175°C).
2. In a bowl, combine the chopped nuts, granulated sugar, ground cinnamon, and ground cloves.

Mix well to ensure the nuts are evenly coated with the sugar and spices.

3. Brush a baking dish with melted butter to prevent the baklava from sticking.

4. Place a sheet of phyllo dough in the baking dish and brush it generously with melted butter.

Repeat this process, layering the phyllo sheets and brushing each layer with butter, until you have used half of the phyllo sheets.

5. Spread the nut mixture evenly over the phyllo layers in the baking dish.

6. Continue layering the remaining phyllo sheets on top of the nut mixture, brushing each layer with melted butter.

7. Using a sharp knife, carefully cut the baklava into diamond or square-shaped pieces.

8. Bake the baklava in the preheated oven for about 45-50 minutes, or until golden brown and crispy.

9. While the baklava is baking, prepare the syrup. In a small saucepan, combine the honey, water, and lemon juice.

Heat the mixture over medium heat until it comes to a gentle boil.

Let it simmer for a few minutes, then remove it from the heat and set aside to cool slightly.

10. Once the baklava is done baking, remove it from the oven and immediately pour the warm syrup over the hot baklava, ensuring that the syrup is evenly distributed.

11. Allow the baklava to cool completely in the baking dish before serving.

This will allow the syrup to be absorbed and the flavors to meld together.

12. Serve the baklava at room temperature, and store any leftovers in an airtight container.

Enjoy the rich and sweet flavors of homemade baklava as a delightful treat from your Middle Eastern culinary adventure!

Section 3: Israeli Falafel and Hummus

Israeli cuisine is influenced by various cultures and is known for its fresh ingredients and vibrant flavors.

Explore the world of falafel, crispy deep-fried balls made from ground chickpeas or fava beans, served in pita bread with an array of fresh vegetables and creamy tahini sauce.

Additionally, learn to prepare creamy and smooth hummus, a popular Middle Eastern dip made from chickpeas, tahini, lemon juice, and garlic, served with warm pita bread or as a spread in sandwiches.

i. Recipe: Isreali Falafel

Ingredients:
- 1 cup dried chickpeas
- 1/2 large onion, roughly chopped
- 1/2 cup fresh parsley leaves
- 1/2 cup fresh cilantro leaves
- 3 cloves garlic
- 1 teaspoon ground cumin
- 1 teaspoon ground coriander
- 1/4 teaspoon cayenne pepper (optional)
- 1 teaspoon salt
- 1/2 teaspoon baking powder
- 4-6 tablespoons all-purpose flour
- Vegetable oil for frying

Instructions:
1. Place the dried chickpeas in a bowl and cover them with water.

Let them soak overnight or for at least 8 hours.

The chickpeas will double in size as they absorb the water.

2. Drain the soaked chickpeas and rinse them thoroughly under cold water.

Make sure to remove any loose skins.

3. In a food processor, add the soaked and drained chickpeas, chopped onion, parsley leaves, cilantro leaves, garlic cloves, ground cumin, ground coriander, cayenne pepper (if desired), salt, and baking powder.

4. Pulse the mixture in the food processor until it becomes a coarse paste.

Scrape down the sides of the food processor as needed to ensure even blending.

5. Transfer the falafel mixture to a bowl and gradually add the all-purpose flour, one tablespoon at a time, mixing well after each addition.

The flour helps bind the mixture together.

Add enough flour until the mixture holds its shape when formed into balls.

6. Cover the falafel mixture and refrigerate it for at least 1 hour.

Chilling the mixture helps it firm up and makes it easier to shape.

7. Heat vegetable oil in a deep frying pan or pot to a temperature of about 350°F (175°C).

8. While the oil is heating, shape the falafel mixture into small patties or balls, about 1 to 1 1/2 inches in diameter.

9. Carefully place the falafel patties or balls into the hot oil, frying them in batches to avoid overcrowding the pan.

Fry them for about 3-4 minutes per side, or until they are golden brown and crispy.

10. Once cooked, remove the falafel from the oil using a slotted spoon and place them on a paper towel-lined plate to drain excess oil.

11. Serve the falafel warm, either as a standalone snack or stuffed inside pita bread with your favorite toppings and sauces, such as tahini sauce, cucumber, tomatoes, and pickles.

Enjoy the delicious and flavorful Israeli falafel as a popular street food or as part of a satisfying meal!

ii. Recipe: Isreali Hummus

Ingredients:

- 1 can (15 ounces) chickpeas, drained and rinsed
- 1/4 cup tahini (sesame paste)
- 3 tablespoons fresh lemon juice
- 2 cloves garlic, minced
- 1/4 cup olive oil
- 1/2 teaspoon ground cumin
- Salt, to taste
- Ice water, as needed
- Paprika and olive oil, for garnish
- Optional toppings: chopped parsley, paprika, or pine nuts

Instructions:
1. In a food processor, combine the chickpeas, tahini, lemon juice, minced garlic, olive oil, ground cumin, and a pinch of salt.

2. Process the mixture until smooth and creamy. If the mixture is too thick, add ice water, a tablespoon at a time, and continue processing until desired consistency is achieved.

3. Taste the hummus and adjust the seasoning, adding more salt, lemon juice, or garlic if desired.

4. Transfer the hummus to a serving bowl.

Create a well in the center with the back of a spoon.

5. Drizzle olive oil over the top of the hummus and sprinkle with paprika for garnish.

6. Optionally, you can also top the hummus with chopped parsley or toasted pine nuts for added flavor and texture.

7. Serve the Israeli hummus with warm pita bread, fresh vegetables, or as a spread in sandwiches and wraps.

Israeli hummus is known for its creamy texture and tangy flavor, often achieved by using generous amounts of tahini and lemon juice.

It is a versatile and popular dish that can be enjoyed as a dip, a spread, or as part of a mezze platter.

Section 4: Iranian Kabobs and Tahdig

Iranian cuisine is characterized by its aromatic spices, fragrant rice, and succulent kabobs.

Get into the art of marinating and grilling flavorful kabobs, whether it's juicy beef, tender chicken, or delicious lamb.

Additionally, explore the technique of making tahdig, a crispy and golden crust that forms at the bottom of the rice pot, adding a delightful crunch to the fluffy rice.

Get ready to explore the culinary treasures of this diverse and flavorful region.

i. Recipe: Iranian Kabobs

Ingredients:

- 1 lb (450 g) boneless meat (such as beef, lamb, or chicken), cut into cubes
- 1 large onion, finely chopped
- 4 cloves garlic, minced
- 2 tablespoons olive oil
- 2 tablespoons plain yogurt
- 1 tablespoon lemon juice
- 1 teaspoon ground turmeric
- 1 teaspoon ground cumin
- 1 teaspoon ground paprika
- 1/2 teaspoon ground black pepper
- 1/2 teaspoon ground cinnamon
- Salt, to taste
- Skewers (metal or soaked wooden skewers)

Instructions:

1. In a bowl, combine the chopped onion, minced garlic, olive oil, plain yogurt, lemon juice, ground turmeric, ground cumin, ground paprika, ground black pepper, ground cinnamon, and salt.

2. Add the cubed meat to the marinade mixture and mix well to ensure all the meat pieces are coated.

Cover the bowl and let it marinate in the refrigerator for at least 2 hours or overnight for the flavors to develop.

3. Preheat the grill or grill pan to medium-high heat.

4. Thread the marinated meat onto skewers, leaving a small space between each piece.

5. Grill the kabobs for about 8-10 minutes, turning occasionally, until the meat is cooked through and slightly charred on the outside.

Cooking time may vary depending on the thickness of the meat and desired doneness.

6. Once cooked, remove the kabobs from the grill and let them rest for a few minutes before serving.

7. Serve the Iranian kabobs hot with rice, grilled vegetables, or flatbread.

Optionally, you can garnish with fresh herbs, such as parsley or mint, for added freshness and flavor.

Iranian kabobs are known for their aromatic spices and tender, juicy meat.

The marinade adds depth of flavor and helps to tenderize the meat.

These kabobs are traditionally grilled to perfection and enjoyed as a main course alongside various accompaniments.

ii. Recipe: Iranian tahdig

Ingredients:

- 2 cups long-grain basmati rice
- 4 tablespoons vegetable oil
- 1/4 teaspoon ground saffron (dissolved in 2 tablespoons of hot water)
- Salt, to taste
- Optional toppings: sliced potatoes, sliced bread, or yogurt

Instructions:
1. Rinse the rice under cold water until the water runs clear.

Soak the rice in cold water for about 30 minutes, then drain.

2. In a large non-stick pot, heat 3 tablespoons of vegetable oil over medium heat.

Add the soaked and drained rice to the pot and spread it evenly.

3. Drizzle the dissolved saffron evenly over the rice.

Season with salt to taste.

4. Create small holes in the rice using the end of a wooden spoon.

This will allow steam to escape and create a crispy bottom layer.

5. Cover the pot with a clean kitchen towel or a layer of aluminum foil, then place the lid on top to create a tight seal.

This helps to trap the steam and create a crispy crust.

6. Reduce the heat to low and let the rice cook undisturbed for about 30-40 minutes, or until the rice is fully cooked and the bottom layer is golden brown and crispy.

7. In a separate small saucepan, heat the remaining 1 tablespoon of vegetable oil.

Once hot, carefully pour the hot oil over the rice, focusing on the edges to help loosen the crispy bottom layer.

8. To serve, gently fluff the rice with a fork, being careful not to break the crispy crust.

Serve the tahdig as a side dish with your favorite Iranian stews, grilled meats, or vegetables.

9. Optional: For added flavor and variety, you can layer sliced potatoes or bread at the bottom of the pot before adding the rice.

This creates different variations of tahdig.

10. You can also serve tahdig with a dollop of plain yogurt on top for a creamy and tangy complement to the crispy rice.

Iranian tahdig is a beloved dish known for its crispy, golden-brown crust and fluffy rice.

It is typically served as a side dish and adds a delightful texture and flavor to any meal.

The saffron-infused rice and the crispy bottom layer create a unique and delicious combination.

Enjoy the tahdig alongside your favorite Iranian dishes for a memorable culinary experience.

Chapter 8: Oceanic Tastes

Introduction to Oceanic Cuisine

Oceanic cuisine encompasses a diverse range of flavors and culinary traditions from the countries and regions surrounding the Pacific Ocean.

From the sizzling barbecues of Australia to the traditional feasts of New Zealand and the vibrant flavors of Hawaiian and Polynesian dishes, Oceanic cuisine is a fusion of indigenous ingredients, cultural influences, and unique cooking techniques.

In this chapter, we will explore some of the iconic dishes from Australia, New Zealand, Hawaii, and Polynesia, inviting you to experience the delightful flavors of the Pacific.

Section 1: Australian barbecue and Pavlova

The Australian barbecue, often referred to as a "barbie," is a beloved tradition that brings friends and families together.

It is a celebration of outdoor cooking, where meats, seafood, and vegetables are grilled to perfection.

Accompanied by fresh salads, condiments, and a laid-back atmosphere, the Australian barbecue captures the essence of Australian culture.

i. Recipe: Australian Barbecue

Ingredients:
- 2 pounds (900g) of beef steak (such as ribeye, sirloin, or flank steak)

- 2 tablespoons olive oil
- 2 cloves garlic, minced
- 1 tablespoon Worcestershire sauce
- 1 tablespoon soy sauce
- Salt and black pepper, to taste

Instructions:
1. Preheat your grill to medium-high heat.

2. In a small bowl, whisk together the olive oil, minced garlic, Worcestershire sauce, and soy sauce to make a marinade.

3. Place the beef steak in a shallow dish and pour the marinade over it, making sure it is well-coated.

Allow the steak to marinate for at least 30 minutes, or refrigerate overnight for enhanced flavor.

4. Season the marinated steak with salt and black pepper on both sides.

5. Place the steak on the preheated grill and cook for about 4-6 minutes per side, or until desired doneness.

For a medium-rare steak, aim for an internal temperature of 130-135°F (55-57°C).

6. Remove the steak from the grill and let it rest for a few minutes before slicing.

7. Slice the steak against the grain into thin strips and serve hot.

8. Optional: Serve the grilled steak with a side of barbecue sauce, grilled vegetables, and a fresh salad.

Enjoy the delicious flavors of Australian barbecue, where the juicy and tender steak is the star of the meal.

The marinade enhances the natural flavors of the beef while adding a savory and slightly tangy touch.

Whether you're hosting a backyard gathering or enjoying a casual weeknight dinner, this Australian barbecue recipe is sure to be a crowd-pleaser.

ii. Recipe: Pavlova

Ingredients:
- 4 large egg whites, at room temperature
- 1 cup caster sugar
- 1 teaspoon cornstarch
- 1 teaspoon white vinegar
- 1/2 teaspoon vanilla extract
- 1 cup heavy cream
- Fresh fruits (such as strawberries, kiwi, and passion fruit) for topping

Instructions:
1. Preheat the oven to 250°F (120°C). Line a baking sheet with parchment paper.

2. In a clean, dry mixing bowl, beat the egg whites using an electric mixer on medium speed until soft peaks form.

3. Gradually add the sugar, one tablespoon at a time, while continuing to beat the egg whites on medium-high speed.

Beat until the mixture is thick, glossy, and the sugar has dissolved.

4. Reduce the speed to low and add the cornstarch, vinegar, and vanilla extract.

Mix until just combined.

5. Spoon the meringue mixture onto the prepared baking sheet, shaping it into a round or oval shape with slightly raised edges.

6. Place the pavlova in the preheated oven and bake for 1 hour or until the outside is crisp and dry.

The center should remain soft and marshmallow-like.

7. Once baked, turn off the oven and leave the pavlova inside to cool completely.

This will help prevent cracking.

8. Whip the heavy cream until soft peaks form.

Spread the whipped cream over the cooled pavlova.

9. Top the pavlova with an assortment of fresh fruits, such as sliced strawberries, kiwi, and passion fruit.

10. Serve the pavlova immediately and enjoy the delightful combination of the crisp meringue, creamy whipped cream, and juicy fruits.

The pavlova is a quintessential Australian dessert named after the Russian ballerina, Anna Pavlova.

It is a sweet meringue-based dessert with a crisp outer shell and a soft, marshmallow-like interior.

Topped with whipped cream and a variety of fresh fruits, the pavlova is a delightful treat that showcases the vibrant flavors of Australia.

Section 2: New Zealand Hangi and Kiwi Pies

New Zealand's traditional Hangi is a unique cooking method that involves burying food in an underground pit with heated rocks.

This slow-cooking technique infuses the food with smoky flavors and creates tender, succulent meats and vegetables.

Kiwi Pies, on the other hand, are handheld savory pastries filled with delicious combinations of meats, vegetables, and rich gravy.

i. Recipe: New Zealand Hangi

Ingredients:
- 1 whole chicken, cleaned and giblets removed
- 2 pounds (900g) pork shoulder or lamb shoulder, cut into large pieces
- 2 pounds (900g) sweet potatoes, peeled and cut into chunks
- 2 pounds (900g) potatoes, peeled and cut into chunks
- 2 pounds (900g) carrots, peeled and cut into chunks
- 2 onions, peeled and quartered
- 4 cups (950ml) chicken or vegetable broth
- 2 tablespoons melted butter or oil
- Salt, to taste
- Ground black pepper, to taste

Instructions:
1. Preheat your outdoor fire pit or traditional hangi pit by burning wood until it turns into hot coals.

You can also use a large covered barbecue with indirect heat.

2. Line the bottom of the hangi pit or barbecue with clean rocks or stones.

3. In a large pot or Dutch oven, bring the chicken broth to a boil. Add the chicken, pork or lamb, and season with salt and pepper.

Cook for about 20 minutes, or until the meats are partially cooked.

4. Remove the meats from the pot and set aside. Reserve the broth for later use.

5. Place the sweet potatoes, potatoes, carrots, and onions on top of the hot rocks in the hangi pit or barbecue.

Arrange the partially cooked meats on top of the vegetables.

6. Cover the meats and vegetables with damp cloth or banana leaves to keep them moist.

7. Pour the reserved broth over the meats and vegetables.

The broth will create steam that will cook the food.

8. Cover the hangi pit or barbecue with a lid or a layer of aluminum foil, ensuring it is tightly sealed to trap the steam.

9. Cook the hangi for about 2-3 hours, or until the meats are tender and the vegetables are cooked through.

10. Carefully remove the lid or foil and check if the meats and vegetables are fully cooked.

If needed, continue cooking for a bit longer.

11. Remove the meats and vegetables from the hangi pit or barbecue.

Brush them with melted butter or oil to add shine and flavor.

12. Serve the New Zealand Hangi hot, family-style, allowing everyone to help themselves to the meats and vegetables.

The New Zealand Hangi is a traditional Maori method of cooking that results in tender meats and flavorful vegetables.

The combination of steam and heat creates a unique and delicious smoky flavor.

This communal cooking style is perfect for gatherings and special occasions, bringing people together to enjoy a meal that is rich in cultural heritage and flavor.

ii. Recipe: Kiwi Pies

Ingredients:
- 2 sheets of pre-made puff pastry
- 1 tablespoon olive oil
- 1 onion, finely chopped
- 2 cloves of garlic, minced
- 1 pound (450g) ground beef or lamb
- 1 carrot, finely chopped
- 1 celery stalk, finely chopped
- 1 cup (240ml) beef or vegetable broth
- 2 tablespoons tomato paste
- 1 tablespoon Worcestershire sauce
- 1 teaspoon dried thyme
- Salt, to taste
- Ground black pepper, to taste
- 1 egg, beaten (for egg wash)

Instructions:
1. Preheat your oven to 400°F (200°C).

2. Heat the olive oil in a large skillet over medium heat.

Add the onion and garlic, and sauté until they become fragrant and translucent.

3. Add the ground beef or lamb to the skillet and cook until it is browned and cooked through.

Break up any clumps with a spoon.

4. Stir in the carrot, celery, beef or vegetable broth, tomato paste, Worcestershire sauce, dried thyme, salt, and pepper.

Cook for an additional 5-7 minutes, or until the vegetables are tender and the flavors are well combined.

Remove from heat and let the filling cool slightly.

5. Roll out the puff pastry sheets on a lightly floured surface.

Cut out rounds or squares, depending on the size of the pies you prefer.

6. Spoon a generous amount of the meat filling onto one half of each pastry round or square, leaving a small border around the edges.

7. Fold the other half of the pastry over the filling to create a half-moon shape.

Use a fork to press and seal the edges of the pies.

8. Place the pies on a baking sheet lined with parchment paper.

Brush the tops of the pies with the beaten egg, which will give them a golden brown color when baked.

9. Bake the pies in the preheated oven for about 20-25 minutes, or until the pastry is puffed and golden brown.

10. Remove the pies from the oven and let them cool slightly before serving.

Kiwi Pies are a popular savory pastry dish in New Zealand, often enjoyed as a quick and satisfying meal.

The flaky puff pastry encases a flavorful meat filling, creating a delicious handheld treat.

These pies can be made with various fillings, but the classic version with ground beef or lamb, along with vegetables and aromatic seasonings, is a favorite among Kiwis.

Enjoy these Kiwi Pies as a snack, lunch, or dinner option, either on-the-go or at home.

Section 3: Hawaiian Poke and Huli Huli Chicken

Hawaii is known for its vibrant culinary scene, and two standout dishes are Poke and Huli Huli Chicken.

Poke is a refreshing raw fish salad typically made with marinated chunks of fresh fish, such as ahi tuna or salmon, mixed with various seasonings and toppings.

It is a staple in Hawaiian cuisine and has gained popularity worldwide for its delicious flavors and vibrant presentation.

Huli Huli Chicken, on the other hand, is a Hawaiian-style grilled chicken that is marinated in a tangy and sweet sauce, resulting in juicy and flavorful meat with a slightly caramelized exterior.

i. Recipe: Hawaiian Poke

Ingredients:
- 1 pound (450g) sushi-grade fresh fish (such as tuna or salmon), cubed
- 1/4 cup soy sauce
- 1 tablespoon sesame oil
- 1 tablespoon rice vinegar
- 1 tablespoon honey or brown sugar
- 1 teaspoon grated fresh ginger
- 1 clove garlic, minced
- 1 green onion, thinly sliced
- 1/2 teaspoon toasted sesame seeds
- Optional toppings: sliced avocado, seaweed salad, diced cucumber, chopped scallions

Instructions:
1. In a mixing bowl, combine the soy sauce, sesame oil, rice vinegar, honey or brown sugar, grated ginger, and minced garlic.

Whisk well to combine and dissolve the sweetener.

2. Add the cubed fresh fish to the bowl and gently toss it in the marinade until all the pieces are coated.

Cover the bowl with plastic wrap and refrigerate for at least 30 minutes to allow the flavors to meld.

3. Before serving, give the poke a quick stir to redistribute the marinade.

Taste and adjust the seasoning if needed.

4. Sprinkle the sliced green onion and toasted sesame seeds over the poke, and gently toss to incorporate them.

5. Serve the Hawaiian poke in bowls, either on its own or over a bed of steamed rice.

You can also add optional toppings such as sliced avocado, seaweed salad, diced cucumber, or chopped scallions to enhance the flavors and textures.

Hawaiian Poke is a refreshing and flavorful raw fish salad that originates from Hawaii.

It typically consists of fresh, sushi-grade fish, marinated in a combination of soy sauce, sesame oil, and other seasonings.

The result is a dish bursting with umami flavors and a hint of sweetness.

The marinade helps to tenderize the fish and infuse it with delicious taste.

Hawaiian Poke is often enjoyed as an appetizer or a light meal, and it has gained popularity worldwide for its simplicity and vibrant flavors.

Feel free to customize your poke bowl with your favorite toppings and enjoy a taste of Hawaii right in your own home.

ii. Recipe: Huli Huli Chicken

Ingredients:
- 4 bone-in, skin-on chicken thighs
- 1/2 cup pineapple juice
- 1/4 cup soy sauce
- 1/4 cup ketchup
- 1/4 cup brown sugar
- 2 tablespoons rice vinegar

- 2 cloves garlic, minced
- 1 tablespoon grated ginger
- 1 teaspoon sesame oil
- Salt and pepper to taste
- Optional garnish: sliced green onions, sesame seeds

Instructions:
1. In a bowl, combine the pineapple juice, soy sauce, ketchup, brown sugar, rice vinegar, minced garlic, grated ginger, sesame oil, salt, and pepper.

Whisk until the ingredients are well combined.

2. Place the chicken thighs in a large zip-top bag or a shallow dish.

Pour the marinade over the chicken, making sure to coat each piece evenly.

Seal the bag or cover the dish with plastic wrap and refrigerate for at least 2 hours, or preferably overnight, to allow the flavors to penetrate the chicken.

3. Preheat your grill to medium-high heat.

Remove the chicken from the marinade, allowing any excess marinade to drip off.

4. Grill the chicken thighs for about 5-6 minutes per side, or until they reach an internal temperature of 165°F (74°C).

Baste the chicken with the remaining marinade during the last few minutes of grilling, ensuring a flavorful glaze.

5. Once cooked, transfer the chicken to a serving platter and let it rest for a few minutes.

Garnish with sliced green onions and sesame seeds, if desired.

6. Serve the Huli Huli Chicken hot with your favorite side dishes, such as steamed rice or grilled vegetables.

The chicken will be tender, juicy, and infused with the sweet and tangy flavors of the marinade.

Huli Huli Chicken is a popular Hawaiian dish known for its delicious sweet and savory glaze.

The marinade, made with pineapple juice, soy sauce, ketchup, brown sugar, and other ingredients, imparts a tropical flavor to the chicken.

The term "huli huli" means "turn turn" in Hawaiian, referring to the grilling technique of constantly turning the chicken on the grill to ensure even cooking and to achieve a caramelized exterior.

Grilling the chicken thighs gives them a smoky char and locks in the juicy tenderness.

The basting with the marinade during grilling adds an extra layer of flavor and creates a mouthwatering glaze.

The result is succulent, flavorful chicken with a perfect balance of sweetness and tanginess.

Huli Huli Chicken is a fantastic dish for backyard barbecues, summer parties, or any occasion when you want to savor the flavors of Hawaii.

Serve it as a main course with your favorite side dishes, or slice it and use it in sandwiches or salads.

Enjoy the taste of the islands with this irresistible Huli Huli Chicken recipe.

Section 4: Polynesian Luau and Samoan Palusami

Polynesian cuisine is deeply rooted in traditional cultural practices and celebrations.

The Polynesian Luau is a festive feast that showcases a variety of dishes, including roasted meats, seafood, tropical fruits, and traditional side dishes.

It is a communal gathering where people come together to enjoy good food, music, and dance.

Samoan Palusami, a traditional dish from Samoa, consists of taro leaves filled with a rich and creamy mixture of coconut milk, onions, and seasonings.

The parcels are then wrapped in banana leaves and cooked until tender, creating a flavorful and comforting dish.

i. Recipe: Polynesian Luau (Kalua Pig)

Ingredients:
- 5-6 pounds pork shoulder or pork butt, bone-in
- 2 tablespoons sea salt
- 2 tablespoons liquid smoke
- 6-8 large banana leaves (optional)
- Aluminum foil
- Optional garnish: pineapple slices, fresh herbs

Instructions:
1. Preheat your oven to 325°F (163°C).

2. Rinse the pork shoulder or pork butt under cold water and pat it dry with paper towels.

3. Rub the sea salt all over the pork, ensuring even coverage.

Let it sit for a few minutes to allow the salt to penetrate the meat.

4. Drizzle the liquid smoke over the pork, spreading it evenly.

The liquid smoke will infuse a smoky flavor into the meat, simulating the traditional underground pit cooking method.

5. If using banana leaves, lay them flat on a large baking dish or roasting pan, creating a bed for the pork.

Place the seasoned pork on top of the banana leaves.

If you don't have banana leaves, you can skip this step and proceed to the next.

6. Wrap the pork tightly in several layers of aluminum foil, ensuring it is fully enclosed.

This will help trap the moisture and create a steamy cooking environment.

7. Place the wrapped pork in the preheated oven and roast for about 4-5 hours, or until the meat is tender and easily pulls apart with a fork.

The cooking time may vary depending on the size and thickness of the pork.

8. Once the pork is fully cooked, carefully remove it from the oven and let it rest for a few minutes.

Unwrap the foil and transfer the pork to a cutting board.

9. Shred the pork using two forks, discarding any excess fat or bone. The meat should be moist and tender.

10. Serve the Kalua Pig as the centerpiece of your Polynesian Luau.

Arrange the shredded pork on a platter and garnish with pineapple slices and fresh herbs, if desired.

The Polynesian Luau, specifically the Kalua Pig, is a traditional Hawaiian dish often prepared for festive gatherings and celebrations.

It involves slow-roasting a whole pig in an underground oven called an "imu," but this recipe provides a simplified version that can be made in a home oven.

The pork shoulder or pork butt is seasoned with sea salt and liquid smoke, which gives it a rich, smoky flavor reminiscent of the traditional cooking method.

Banana leaves, if available, can be used to enhance the flavor and presentation.

The pork is then wrapped tightly in foil and slow-roasted for several hours until it becomes tender and easily shreddable.

The result is succulent, flavorful pulled pork that can be enjoyed as the main dish of your Polynesian Luau. Serve it with traditional Hawaiian sides like poi, macaroni salad, and tropical fruits to create an authentic and festive meal.

The Kalua Pig is not only delicious but also a symbol of community, celebration, and the spirit of the Polynesian culture.

Whether you're hosting a Hawaiian-themed party or simply craving a taste of the islands, the Polynesian Luau with its flavorful Kalua Pig is sure to delight your guests and transport them to the tropical paradise of Polynesia.

ii. Recipe: Samoan Palusami

Ingredients:
- 2 bundles of taro leaves
- 1 can of coconut cream
- 1 onion, finely chopped
- 2 cloves of garlic, minced
- 1 tablespoon lemon juice
- Salt, to taste

Instructions:
1. Wash the taro leaves thoroughly and remove any tough stems.

Cut the leaves into small pieces.

2. In a large pot, bring water to a boil.

Blanch the taro leaves in the boiling water for about 5 minutes, until they become wilted and tender.

Drain the leaves and set them aside.

3. In a separate bowl, combine the coconut cream, chopped onion, minced garlic, lemon juice, and salt.

Mix well to incorporate the flavors.

4. Preheat your oven to 350°F (175°C).

5. Take a deep baking dish or casserole and line the bottom with a layer of taro leaves.

6. Pour a portion of the coconut cream mixture over the leaves, spreading it evenly.

Repeat this process, layering the remaining taro leaves and coconut cream mixture.

7. Cover the baking dish with aluminum foil and place it in the preheated oven.

Bake for approximately 1 hour, or until the taro leaves are tender and the coconut cream has thickened.

8. Once cooked, remove the Palusami from the oven and let it cool slightly before serving.

9. Palusami is traditionally enjoyed as a side dish or accompaniment to other Samoan dishes.

It pairs well with roasted meats, fish, or rice.

Palusami is a traditional Samoan dish made with taro leaves and coconut cream.

It is a delicious and flavorful dish that reflects the rich culinary heritage of Samoa.

The taro leaves are blanched to soften them and then layered with a mixture of coconut cream, onion, garlic, lemon juice, and salt.

The dish is then baked, allowing the flavors to meld together and the coconut cream to thicken.

The result is a creamy and aromatic dish with tender taro leaves and a rich coconut flavor.

The Palusami can be served as a side dish or as part of a larger Samoan feast.

It complements various main dishes such as roasted meats, fish, or rice, adding a touch of tropical indulgence to the meal.

Palusami holds cultural significance in Samoan cuisine and is often prepared for special occasions, gatherings, and family celebrations.

It represents the warmth, hospitality, and communal spirit of the Samoan people.

Sharing a meal of Palusami creates a sense of togetherness and unity, as friends and family gather around the table to enjoy the flavors of Samoa.

Whether you're exploring the diverse cuisine of the Pacific Islands or simply looking to experience a taste of Samoa, the Palusami is a delightful and satisfying dish that showcases the unique flavors and culinary traditions of the Samoan culture.

In this chapter, we have explored the diverse flavors of Oceanic cuisine, from the sizzling Australian barbecues to the traditional feasts of New Zealand and the vibrant Hawaiian and Polynesian dishes.

Each dish reflects the unique cultural heritage and culinary traditions of its respective region, inviting you to embark on a culinary journey through the Pacific and experience the rich flavors and vibrant cultures of the Oceanic countries.

Note: The recipes provided are simplified versions and can be customized based on personal preferences and dietary restrictions.

Chapter 9: Fusion Fare

Introduction:
Fusion Fare is a culinary journey that embraces the art of blending flavors from different cuisines around the world.

It celebrates the creativity and innovation in the kitchen, where traditional ingredients and cooking techniques are combined with modern twists and global inspirations.

In this chapter, we explore the exciting world of Fusion Fare, where boundaries are pushed, and new culinary possibilities emerge.

Blending Flavors from Around the World:
Fusion cuisine is all about bringing together ingredients, techniques, and flavors from different culinary traditions to create harmonious and unique dishes.

It's a melting pot of cultures, where chefs and home cooks experiment with combinations that may seem unconventional but result in surprising and delightful flavor profiles.

From Asian-infused tacos to Mediterranean-inspired sushi rolls, Fusion Fare invites us to explore new tastes and textures that transcend traditional boundaries.

Creative Recipes and Innovations:
In Fusion Fare, creativity knows no limits.

Chefs and home cooks alike are constantly pushing the boundaries of culinary innovation, combining ingredients and techniques in unexpected ways.

It's a playground for culinary experimentation, where flavors from different cuisines intertwine to create exciting and memorable dishes.

From deconstructed classics to reinvented comfort foods, Fusion Fare offers a vibrant canvas for culinary expression.

In this chapter, you'll find a collection of creative recipes that showcase the art of fusion cooking.

Each dish takes inspiration from multiple culinary traditions, combining ingredients and techniques to create unique and tantalizing flavors.

From Asian-Mexican fusion to Mediterranean-Asian fusion, these recipes will take your taste buds on a thrilling adventure.

Whether you're a seasoned chef or a curious home cook, Fusion Fare invites you to step outside your culinary comfort zone and explore the world of possibilities that emerge when different flavors and cultures collide.

Get ready to embark on a culinary journey that celebrates diversity, creativity, and the joy of experimenting with food.

Here is a collection of creative recipes that showcase the art of fusion cooking:

1. Sushi Burritos:
  - **Ingredients:**
    - Nori sheets
    - Sushi rice

- Assorted fillings (e.g., avocado, cucumber, crab meat, tempura shrimp)
    - Spicy mayo or sriracha sauce

- **Instructions:**

Spread sushi rice on a nori sheet, layer with fillings, and roll tightly. Slice into burrito-sized pieces and serve with spicy mayo or sriracha sauce.

2. Thai Curry Tacos:
- **Ingredients:**
    - Taco shells or tortillas
    - Thai red or green curry paste
    - Grilled chicken or tofu
    - Fresh vegetables (e.g., shredded cabbage, carrots, cucumbers)
    - Fresh herbs (e.g., cilantro, Thai basil)

- **Instructions:**

Mix the curry paste with grilled chicken or tofu. Fill taco shells with the curry mixture, fresh vegetables, and herbs.

Serve with a squeeze of lime.

3. Korean BBQ Pizza:
- **Ingredients:**
    - Pizza dough
    - Bulgogi (Korean marinated beef)
    - Kimchi
    - Mozzarella cheese
    - Green onions, thinly sliced

- **Instructions:**

Roll out pizza dough and top with bulgogi, kimchi, mozzarella cheese, and green onions.

Bake until the crust is golden and the cheese is melted.

4. Mexican-Asian Fusion Salad:

- **Ingredients:**
  - Mixed greens
  - Grilled shrimp or tofu
  - Avocado, diced
  - Mango, diced
  - Tortilla strips
  - Cilantro-lime dressing

- **Instructions:**

Toss mixed greens with grilled shrimp or tofu, diced avocado, diced mango, and tortilla strips.

Drizzle with cilantro-lime dressing.

5. Indian-Spiced Tacos:

- **Ingredients:**
  - Roti or taco shells
  - Tandoori chicken or paneer
  - Raita (yogurt sauce)
  - Mango chutney
  - Fresh cilantro leaves

- **Instructions:**

Fill roti or taco shells with tandoori chicken or paneer.

Top with raita, mango chutney, and fresh cilantro leaves.

Here are a few more creative fusion recipes for you to explore:

1. Korean-Mexican Bulgogi Tacos:

- **Ingredients:**
  - Corn tortillas
  - Bulgogi (Korean marinated beef)
  - Kimchi slaw (shredded cabbage mixed with kimchi)
  - Sriracha mayo
  - Cilantro, chopped

- **Instructions:**

Fill corn tortillas with bulgogi, kimchi slaw, drizzle with sriracha mayo, and sprinkle with chopped cilantro.

2. Italian-Indian Naan Pizza:

- **Ingredients:**
  - Naan bread
  - Tomato sauce
  - Mozzarella cheese
  - Tandoori chicken or paneer
  - Sliced bell peppers and onions
  - Fresh basil leaves

- **Instructions:**

Spread tomato sauce on naan bread, top with mozzarella cheese, tandoori chicken or paneer, sliced bell peppers and onions.

Bake until the cheese is melted. Garnish with fresh basil leaves.

3. Thai-Mexican Fusion Burritos:

- **Ingredients:**

- Flour tortillas
- Thai green curry paste
- Grilled shrimp or chicken
- Jasmine rice
- Sliced bell peppers and onions
- Fresh cilantro and mint leaves

- Instructions:
Spread Thai green curry paste on a flour tortilla, fill with grilled shrimp or chicken, jasmine rice, sliced bell peppers and onions.

Garnish with fresh cilantro and mint leaves. Roll into a burrito shape.

4. Japanese-Italian Fusion Pasta:

- Ingredients:
- Spaghetti or linguine
- Miso butter sauce (blend miso paste with melted butter)
- Grilled shrimp or scallops
- Roasted cherry tomatoes
- Fresh basil leaves

- Instructions:
Cook pasta according to package instructions.

Toss cooked pasta with miso butter sauce, grilled shrimp or scallops, roasted cherry tomatoes, and fresh basil leaves.

5. Mexican-Indian Fusion Quesadillas:

- Ingredients:
- Flour tortillas
- Tandoori chicken or paneer
- Spicy mango chutney
- Shredded Mexican cheese blend

- Chopped cilantro

- Instructions:
Spread spicy mango chutney on a flour tortilla, top with tandoori chicken or paneer, shredded Mexican cheese blend, and chopped cilantro.

Place another tortilla on top.

Cook in a skillet until the cheese is melted and tortilla is crispy.

Feel free to mix and match flavors, ingredients, and cooking techniques from different cuisines to create your own unique fusion recipes.

The possibilities are endless when it comes to combining the best of different culinary traditions.

Enjoy your culinary adventure!

These are just a few examples of the creative fusion recipes you can explore.

Feel free to experiment with different ingredients, flavors, and cooking techniques to create your own unique fusion dishes.

Let your imagination and taste buds guide you on your culinary journey!

Note: The recipes in this chapter are meant to inspire your own culinary adventures.

Feel free to adapt and personalize them according to your preferences and the ingredients available to you.

Let your imagination run wild as you embrace the spirit of Fusion Fare and create dishes that truly reflect your unique culinary vision.

Enjoy the fusion of flavors and the exciting discoveries.

Chapter 10: Sweet Endings

Introduction:
Indulge your sweet tooth as we explore the world of decadent desserts from different cultures.

In this chapter, we'll dive into a delightful array of cakes, pastries, and treats that will satisfy any dessert lover's cravings.

From classic favorites to unique creations, get ready to embark on a journey of sweetness and delight.

Section 1: Decadent Desserts from Different Cultures
Discover the diverse flavors and techniques used in creating desserts from various corners of the globe.

Each dessert represents a unique cultural tradition, showcasing the artistry and creativity of different culinary heritages.

Prepare to be tempted by an assortment of flavors, textures, and aromas that will transport your taste buds to far-off places.

Desserts from around the world showcase a remarkable range of flavors and techniques, each influenced by the unique cultural traditions and ingredients of their respective regions.

From delicate French pastries to rich Indian sweets, the diversity of desserts reflects the creativity and expertise of different culinary heritages.

Let's explore the diverse flavors and techniques used in creating desserts from various corners of the globe

1. European Delights:

- French Patisserie:
French desserts are known for their elegance and precision.

From flaky croissants to delicate macarons and intricate layered cakes, French patisserie showcases a mastery of technique and a harmonious blend of flavors.

French patisserie is renowned worldwide for its exquisite pastries and delicate creations.

With a focus on precision, technique, and the finest ingredients, French pastry chefs have elevated the art of dessert-making to new heights.

Let's go into the world of French patisserie:

i. - Classic Croissant:
- Ingredients:
Flour, butter, water, yeast, sugar, salt.

- Instructions:
The process involves creating a laminated dough by layering butter between thin layers of dough.

The dough is then rolled, folded, and shaped into crescent shapes before being baked to golden perfection.

ii. - Macarons:

- Ingredients:

Almond flour, powdered sugar, egg whites, granulated sugar, flavorings (such as vanilla, chocolate, or fruit extracts), food coloring.

- Instructions:
Macarons require delicate precision to achieve their characteristic smooth shells and chewy centers.

The almond flour and powdered sugar are sifted and mixed with whipped egg whites, creating a thick batter.

The batter is piped into small rounds and baked until they develop their signature "feet."

iii. - Opera Cake:
- Ingredients:
Almond sponge cake, coffee buttercream, chocolate ganache, coffee syrup.

- Instructions:
The opera cake is made by layering almond sponge cake soaked in coffee syrup with alternating layers of coffee buttercream and chocolate ganache.

The cake is then finished with a smooth chocolate glaze, and the signature diagonal lines are drawn on top.

iv. - Profiteroles:
- Ingredients:
Water, butter, flour, eggs, whipped cream, chocolate sauce.

- Instructions:
Profiteroles are small choux pastry puffs filled with whipped cream and typically served with a drizzle of warm chocolate sauce.

The choux pastry is made by boiling water and butter, then adding flour to form a dough.

Eggs are added to the dough, which is then piped onto a baking sheet and baked until puffed and golden.

French patisserie exemplifies the precision and artistry that goes into creating delicate and delectable desserts.

From the flaky layers of a croissant to the intricate decorations on a macaron, each pastry is a testament to the skill and dedication of French pastry chefs.

Whether enjoyed in a Parisian café or recreated in your own kitchen, French patisserie offers a truly indulgent and unforgettable experience.

Italian Gelato:
Italian gelato is celebrated for its smooth and creamy texture, made with fresh ingredients and intense flavors.

It's churned at a slower speed than traditional ice cream, resulting in a denser and more luscious dessert.

Italian gelato is renowned for its smooth and creamy texture, intense flavors, and vibrant colors.

Unlike traditional ice cream, gelato is churned at a slower speed, incorporating less air, resulting in a denser and more velvety consistency.

Let's explore the world of Italian gelato:

i. - Classic Vanilla Gelato:

  - Ingredients:

Milk, cream, sugar, egg yolks, vanilla bean.

- Instructions:
The base for vanilla gelato is made by heating milk, cream, and sugar until it reaches a simmer.

In a separate bowl, egg yolks are whisked, and the hot milk mixture is slowly poured into the yolks while whisking constantly.

The mixture is then returned to the stovetop and cooked until it thickens.

Finally, the gelato base is strained, cooled, and churned in an ice cream maker to achieve the desired texture.

ii. - Stracciatella Gelato:

- Ingredients:
Milk, cream, sugar, egg yolks, dark chocolate.

- Instructions:
Stracciatella gelato starts with the same base as vanilla gelato.

Once the base is churned, melted dark chocolate is drizzled into the machine during the last few minutes of churning, creating delicate chocolate flakes throughout the gelato.

iii. - Pistachio Gelato:

- Ingredients:
Milk, cream, sugar, egg yolks, pistachio paste.

- Instructions:
Pistachio gelato begins with the same base as vanilla gelato.

To infuse the gelato with the distinctive flavor of pistachios, pistachio paste or ground pistachios are added to the base during the heating process.

The mixture is then cooled, churned, and transformed into a luscious pistachio gelato.

iv. - **Stracciatella Gelato:**

  - **Ingredients:** Milk, cream, sugar, egg yolks, espresso coffee.

  - **Instructions:**
Espresso gelato is made by adding a strong and concentrated espresso coffee to the gelato base during the heating process.

The mixture is then cooled, churned, and transformed into a rich and aromatic gelato with a delightful coffee flavor.

Italian gelato offers a wide range of flavors, from classic favorites like vanilla and chocolate to unique combinations like fruit sorbets and indulgent nut-based varieties.

The craftsmanship and dedication of Italian gelato makers shine through in every spoonful, delivering a delightful and refreshing dessert experience.

Whether enjoyed in a traditional gelateria in Italy or recreated at home, Italian gelato is sure to transport your taste buds to the sun-drenched streets of Italy.

2. Asian Sweet Treats:

  - **Japanese Wagashi:**

These traditional Japanese sweets are often served with tea and feature a delicate balance of sweetness, texture, and seasonal flavors.

Made from ingredients like red bean paste, mochi, and matcha, wagashi reflects the harmony of nature and the beauty of simplicity.

Wagashi is a traditional Japanese confectionery that encompasses a wide variety of sweet treats.

These delicate and beautifully crafted desserts are deeply rooted in Japanese culture and are often enjoyed with tea.

Let's explore the artistry of Japanese Wagashi:

i. - Sakura Mochi:

- **Ingredients**: Sweet glutinous rice, red bean paste, salted cherry blossom leaves.

- **Instructions:**
Sakura mochi is made by steaming sweet glutinous rice and forming it into a flattened shape.

A dollop of sweet red bean paste is placed in the center, and the mochi is carefully wrapped with a salted cherry blossom leaf.

The result is a delightful combination of chewy mochi, creamy red bean filling, and a subtle floral aroma.

ii. - Matcha Dorayaki:

- **Ingredient**s:
Pancake batter, sweet red bean paste, matcha (green tea) powder.

- Instructions:
 Matcha dorayaki is a twist on the traditional dorayaki, which consists of two fluffy pancakes sandwiching a sweet filling.

In this variation, matcha powder is added to the pancake batter, giving it a vibrant green color and a distinct earthy flavor.

The pancakes are cooked until golden brown, filled with sweet red bean paste, and folded in half.

iii. - Yuzu Yokan:

- Ingredients:
Azuki bean paste, agar agar, sugar, yuzu juice.

- Instructions:
Yuzu yokan is a soft and jelly-like dessert made by simmering azuki bean paste, sugar, and yuzu juice until thickened.

Agar agar, a type of seaweed-based gelatin, is then added to set the mixture.

Once cooled and solidified, the yokan is sliced into elegant rectangles and served.

iv. - Taiyaki:

- Ingredients:
Pancake batter, sweet red bean paste.

- Instructions:
Taiyaki is a popular fish-shaped pastry filled with sweet red bean paste.

The pancake-like batter is poured into a fish-shaped mold, and a dollop of red bean paste is added to the center.

The taiyaki is then cooked until golden brown, creating a crispy exterior and a warm, gooey filling.

Wagashi is not only a treat for the taste buds but also a feast for the eyes.

The intricate designs, vibrant colors, and harmonious flavors make Japanese Wagashi a true work of art.

Each wagashi confection reflects the changing seasons, cultural traditions, and the pursuit of balance and harmony in Japanese cuisine.

Whether enjoyed during a tea ceremony or as a sweet indulgence, Japanese Wagashi provides a glimpse into the rich culinary heritage of Japan.

   - Indian Mithai: Indian desserts, known as mithai, are rich in flavors and often made with ingredients like milk, ghee, nuts, and aromatic spices.

From the syrup-soaked gulab jamun to the milk-based rasgulla and the saffron-infused kheer, Indian mithai offers a delightful blend of sweet, creamy, and fragrant flavors.

Indian Mithai:

Mithai, or Indian sweets, hold a special place in Indian cuisine and culture.

These delectable treats are made using a variety of ingredients such as milk, ghee (clarified butter), sugar, nuts, and aromatic spices.

Let's go into the world of Indian Mithai and discover the sweet delights it has to offer:

i. - Gulab Jamun:

- Ingredients:
Milk powder, all-purpose flour, ghee, sugar, rose water, cardamom powder.

- Instructions:
Gulab Jamun is made by combining milk powder, all-purpose flour, and a small amount of ghee to form a dough.

The dough is shaped into small balls, deep-fried until golden brown, and then soaked in a fragrant sugar syrup infused with rose water and cardamom.

The result is soft, syrup-soaked dumplings with a melt-in-your-mouth texture.

ii. - Kaju Katli:
- Ingredients:
Cashew nuts, sugar, ghee, cardamom powder, edible silver foil.

- Instructions:
Kaju Katli is a popular Indian sweet made primarily with ground cashew nuts.

The cashews are ground into a fine powder, mixed with sugar, and cooked with ghee until the mixture thickens.

It is then flavored with cardamom powder and rolled out into thin, diamond-shaped pieces.

Kaju Katli is often adorned with edible silver foil, adding a touch of elegance to this nutty delight.

iii. - Jalebi:

- Ingredients:
All-purpose flour, yogurt, saffron, sugar syrup, ghee for frying.

- Instructions:
Jalebi is a spiral-shaped, deep-fried sweet that is soaked in sugar syrup.

The batter for jalebi is made by fermenting all-purpose flour and yogurt overnight, which gives it a slight tangy flavor.

The batter is then piped into hot ghee in a spiral shape and fried until crispy and golden.

Once fried, the jalebis are soaked in saffron-infused sugar syrup, resulting in a sweet and syrupy treat.

iv. - Rasgulla:

- Ingredients:
Paneer (Indian cottage cheese), sugar, water, cardamom powder, rose water.

- Instructions:
Rasgulla is made by kneading paneer until smooth and then shaping it into small balls.

The balls are cooked in a sugar syrup infused with cardamom and rose water, allowing them to absorb the flavors.

Rasgullas are soft, spongy, and slightly sweet, making them a delightful dessert that is often enjoyed chilled.

Indian Mithai is a testament to the rich culinary heritage of India, and each sweet has its own story and significance.

Whether enjoyed during festive occasions, celebrations, or simply as a sweet indulgence, Indian Mithai brings joy and happiness to every bite.

The diversity of flavors, textures, and aromas in Indian Mithai is a true reflection of the vibrant and diverse culture of India.

3. Middle Eastern Delicacies:

- Turkish Delights:
These gelatinous and sweet treats, known as lokum or Turkish delights, are often flavored with rosewater, citrus, or nuts.

They come in an array of colors and are dusted with powdered sugar, making them an exquisite indulgence.

Turkish Delights, also known as Lokum, are a popular and beloved sweet treat in Turkey and around the world.

These delightful confections have a soft, chewy texture and are often flavored with ingredients such as rosewater, citrus, nuts, and spices.

Let's explore the world of Turkish Delights and discover some of the mouthwatering varieties:

i. - Rosewater Delights:

- Ingredients:
Cornstarch, sugar, water, lemon juice, rosewater, pistachios (optional).

- Instructions:
Rosewater Delights are made by combining cornstarch, sugar, water, and lemon juice in a saucepan.

The mixture is cooked over low heat until it thickens and becomes translucent.

Rosewater is then added to infuse the delicate floral flavor. The mixture is poured into a pan, allowed to set, and then cut into small squares or rectangles.

Optionally, pistachios can be sprinkled on top for added texture and flavor.

ii. - Citrus Delights:

- Ingredients:
Cornstarch, sugar, water, lemon juice, orange zest, powdered sugar for coating.

- Instructions:
Citrus Delights are similar to Rosewater Delights in preparation but feature the bright and tangy flavors of citrus.

Cornstarch, sugar, water, lemon juice, and orange zest are cooked together until thickened.

The mixture is then poured into a pan, allowed to cool and set, and cut into bite-sized pieces.

Before serving, the Delights are coated in powdered sugar for a delightful finishing touch.

iii. - Pistachio Delights:

- Ingredients:
Cornstarch, sugar, water, lemon juice, rosewater, pistachios.

- Instructions:
Pistachio Delights combine the signature chewy texture of Turkish Delights with the nutty goodness of pistachios.

The cornstarch, sugar, water, and lemon juice are cooked until thickened, and then rosewater is added for flavor.

Chopped pistachios are mixed into the mixture for added crunch and taste.

The mixture is poured into a pan, allowed to set, and then cut into squares or rectangles.

Turkish Delights are a delightful treat that is enjoyed on various occasions, including holidays, weddings, and special celebrations.

These flavorful confections offer a combination of unique textures, fragrances, and tastes, making them a beloved sweet indulgence.

Whether you prefer the floral notes of rosewater, the zesty burst of citrus, or the crunch of pistachios,

Turkish Delights are sure to captivate your taste buds and transport you to the enchanting world of Turkish cuisine.

- Arabic Baklava:

Baklava is a famous dessert in Middle Eastern cuisine, featuring layers of crispy phyllo pastry filled with nuts and sweetened with a syrup made of honey or rosewater. Its intricate layers and delightful crunch make it a beloved treat.

Arabic Baklava is a rich and indulgent pastry that is popular in many Middle Eastern countries.

It features layers of thin, flaky pastry filled with a sweet and nutty mixture, often flavored with fragrant ingredients such as rosewater or orange blossom water.

Let's explore the art of making Arabic Baklava with a traditional recipe:

i. - Pistachio Baklava:

- Ingredients:

Phyllo pastry sheets, unsalted butter (melted), pistachios (finely chopped), sugar, lemon juice, rosewater or orange blossom water, honey, cinnamon (optional).

- Instructions:

To make Pistachio Baklava, begin by preheating the oven and preparing the filling. In a bowl, combine the finely chopped pistachios, sugar, lemon juice, rosewater or orange blossom water, and optionally, a pinch of cinnamon for added flavor. Mix well to ensure the filling is evenly coated with the aromatic ingredients.

Next, prepare the phyllo pastry by brushing melted butter between each layer to create a stack.

Place a layer of the buttered phyllo pastry in a baking dish, then spread a generous amount of the pistachio filling over it.

Repeat this process, layering the buttered phyllo pastry and pistachio filling until all the ingredients are used.

Once the layers are complete, use a sharp knife to score the top layer of the Baklava into diamond or square shapes.

This will make it easier to cut the Baklava into individual pieces after baking. Bake the Baklava in the preheated oven until it turns golden brown and crispy.

While the Baklava is still hot from the oven, drizzle honey over the top, allowing it to seep into the layers.

This adds sweetness and a glossy finish to the pastry. Let the Baklava cool completely before serving, allowing the flavors to meld together and the pastry to become even more tender.

Arabic Baklava is a beloved dessert that is often enjoyed with a cup of tea or coffee. Its flaky layers, sweet nutty filling, and fragrant aromas create a delightful combination of flavors and textures.

Whether you're celebrating a special occasion or simply craving a sweet treat,

Arabic Baklava is sure to satisfy your dessert cravings and transport you to the enchanting world of Middle Eastern cuisine.

4. Latin American Sweets:

- Mexican Churros:
Churros are deep-fried pastries coated in cinnamon and sugar, often served with a side of chocolate sauce for dipping.

These crispy delights have a satisfying texture and are a popular street food treat.

Mexican Churros are a popular and beloved treat known for their crispy exterior and soft, doughy interior.

These delicious fried pastries are typically dusted with cinnamon sugar and served with a side of chocolate sauce for dipping.

Let's go into the art of making Mexican Churros with a classic recipe:

- Classic Mexican Churros:
 - Ingredients:
All-purpose flour, water, unsalted butter, granulated sugar, salt, eggs, vegetable oil (for frying), ground cinnamon.

 - Instructions:
To make Classic Mexican Churros, start by combining water, butter, sugar, and salt in a saucepan.

Bring the mixture to a boil, then remove from heat and gradually add the flour while stirring continuously. Mix until a smooth dough forms.

Transfer the dough to a piping bag fitted with a star-shaped nozzle.

Heat vegetable oil in a deep pan or skillet over medium heat.

Pipe strips of dough directly into the hot oil, using scissors or a knife to cut the dough at the desired length.

Fry the churros until they turn golden brown and crispy, then remove them from the oil and drain on a paper towel.

In a separate bowl, combine granulated sugar and ground cinnamon.

Roll the freshly fried churros in the cinnamon sugar mixture until they are evenly coated.

Serve the churros warm, accompanied by a rich and creamy chocolate sauce for dipping.

Mexican Churros are a delightful treat that can be enjoyed at any time of the day.

Their irresistible texture, combined with the warm aroma of cinnamon, creates a truly satisfying dessert experience.

Whether you're indulging in them as a standalone treat or as a sweet ending to a Mexican-inspired meal, Mexican Churros are sure to satisfy your cravings and bring a taste of Mexico to your table.

- Brazilian Brigadeiros:
Brigadeiros are small, bite-sized chocolate truffles made from condensed milk, cocoa powder, and butter. Rolled in sprinkles, these fudgy delights are a staple at Brazilian celebrations.

Brazilian Brigadeiros are delectable chocolate truffles that hold a special place in Brazilian cuisine.

These bite-sized delights are made with condensed milk, cocoa powder, butter, and a touch of sweetness.

They are rolled in chocolate sprinkles, creating a rich and indulgent treat.

Let's explore the process of making Brazilian Brigadeiros with a classic recipe:

- Classic Brazilian Brigadeiros:

- Ingredients:
Sweetened condensed milk, unsweetened cocoa powder, unsalted butter, chocolate sprinkles.

- Instructions:
To make Classic Brazilian Brigadeiros, start by combining sweetened condensed milk, cocoa powder, and butter in a medium saucepan.

Cook the mixture over medium heat, stirring continuously to prevent it from sticking to the bottom of the pan.

Continue cooking until the mixture thickens and pulls away from the sides of the pan, forming a dense and fudgy consistency.

Remove the pan from heat and let the mixture cool to room temperature.

Once cooled, butter your hands or use a spoon to scoop small portions of the mixture and roll them into bite-sized balls.

Roll each brigadeiro in chocolate sprinkles until fully coated.

Place the brigadeiros on a plate or in mini cupcake liners for serving.

Brazilian Brigadeiros are a staple at birthday parties, celebrations, and festive occasions in Brazil.

They offer a delightful combination of creamy, chocolaty goodness that melts in your mouth.

These little chocolate truffles are not only delicious but also easy to make, allowing you to enjoy a taste of Brazil in the comfort of your own home.

Whether you're hosting a gathering or simply treating yourself, Brazilian Brigadeiros are sure to satisfy your sweet tooth and bring a touch of Brazilian flair to your dessert table.

These are just a few examples of the diverse flavors and techniques used in creating desserts from different corners of the globe.

 Each region brings its own unique twist, showcasing the local ingredients, cultural influences, and culinary expertise that make desserts a true global delight.

Whether you have a sweet tooth or a passion for culinary exploration, the world of desserts offers endless possibilities for indulgence and discovery.

Section 2: Cakes, Pastries, and Treats
Indulge in the world of cakes, pastries, and treats that are beloved across different cultures.

From delicate pastries to rich and moist cakes, this section will showcase a wide variety of sweet delights.

Whether you prefer something light and airy or rich and decadent, there's a dessert here to satisfy every palate.

i. - Recipe 1: Tiramisu

- Origin: Italy
- Description: This classic Italian dessert features layers of coffee-soaked ladyfingers and creamy mascarpone cheese. Topped with a dusting of cocoa powder, it's a heavenly combination of flavors and textures.

Tiramisu is a classic Italian dessert known for its layers of espresso-soaked ladyfingers, rich mascarpone cream, and a dusting of cocoa powder.

It's a heavenly treat that combines the flavors of coffee and cream in a delightful way.

Let's dive into the recipe for this indulgent dessert:

- **Recipe: Tiramisu**
  - **Ingredients:**
    - 24 ladyfingers
    - 1 ½ cups strong brewed coffee, cooled
    - ½ cup rum or coffee liqueur (optional)
    - 1 cup mascarpone cheese
    - ½ cup granulated sugar
    - 2 cups heavy cream
    - 1 teaspoon vanilla extract
    - Cocoa powder, for dusting

- **Instructions:**
  1. In a shallow dish, combine the cooled coffee and rum or coffee liqueur (if using).

  2. In a mixing bowl, beat the mascarpone cheese and granulated sugar until smooth and creamy.

  3. In a separate bowl, whip the heavy cream and vanilla extract until stiff peaks form.

4. Gently fold the whipped cream into the mascarpone mixture until well combined.

5. Dip each ladyfinger into the coffee mixture, ensuring they are soaked but not soggy.

Place them in a single layer in the bottom of a rectangular serving dish.

6. Spread half of the mascarpone cream mixture over the soaked ladyfingers.

7. Repeat the layers with another layer of soaked ladyfingers and the remaining mascarpone cream mixture.

8. Dust the top layer with cocoa powder.

9. Cover the dish with plastic wrap and refrigerate for at least 4 hours or overnight to allow the flavors to meld and the dessert to set.

10. Before serving, dust with an additional layer of cocoa powder.

Tiramisu is best enjoyed chilled, allowing the flavors to blend together and the ladyfingers to soften slightly. It's a perfect dessert for any occasion, and its elegant presentation makes it a showstopper on the table.

With its creamy, coffee-infused layers, Tiramisu is sure to impress your guests and satisfy your sweet cravings. Buon appetito!

ii. - Recipe : Baklava
- Origin: Middle East

- Description: This Middle Eastern treat is made with layers of flaky phyllo pastry, butter, and a sweet and nutty filling, typically consisting of chopped nuts, honey, and spices.

Each bite is a delightful mix of crunch and sweetness.

Baklava is a delightful sweet pastry that hails from the Middle East and Mediterranean region.

It features layers of crisp phyllo dough filled with a spiced nut mixture and soaked in a sweet syrup.

Let's explore the recipe for this irresistible treat:

- Recipe: Baklava
- Ingredients:
- 1 package of phyllo dough (16 oz)
- 1 ½ cups of unsalted butter, melted
- 2 cups of mixed nuts (such as walnuts, pistachios, and almonds), finely chopped
- 1 teaspoon ground cinnamon
- ½ teaspoon ground cloves
- 1 cup granulated sugar
- 1 cup water
- 1 tablespoon lemon juice
- 1 teaspoon rose water (optional)

- Instructions:
1. Preheat your oven to 350°F (175°C) and grease a baking dish.

2. In a bowl, combine the chopped nuts, cinnamon, and cloves. Set aside.

3. Unroll the phyllo dough and cover it with a damp towel to prevent it from drying out.

4. Brush the bottom of the baking dish with melted butter.

5. Place a sheet of phyllo dough in the dish and brush it with melted butter.

Repeat this process, layering 6 to 8 sheets of phyllo dough.

6. Sprinkle a generous amount of the nut mixture evenly over the phyllo dough.

7. Repeat the layering process with more phyllo dough and melted butter, followed by the nut mixture.

Continue until all the nut mixture is used, ending with a layer of phyllo dough on top.

8. Using a sharp knife, carefully cut the baklava into diamond or square-shaped pieces.

9. Bake the baklava in the preheated oven for about 45-50 minutes, or until it turns golden brown and crispy.

10. While the baklava is baking, prepare the syrup. In a saucepan, combine the granulated sugar, water, lemon juice, and rose water (if using).

Bring the mixture to a boil, then reduce the heat and let it simmer for 10-15 minutes until the syrup thickens slightly.

11. Remove the baklava from the oven and immediately pour the warm syrup over it, ensuring it is evenly distributed.

12. Allow the baklava to cool completely before serving.

This will allow the flavors to meld and the syrup to be absorbed by the layers.

Baklava is best enjoyed at room temperature or slightly warm.

The combination of the crisp, flaky phyllo layers with the sweet and nutty filling creates a heavenly dessert experience.

Serve it as a delightful treat for special occasions or as a sweet ending to a memorable meal.

Enjoy the rich flavors of this beloved Middle Eastern pastry!

iii. - Recipe: Matcha Green Tea Cake
  - Origin: Japan
  - Description: This elegant Japanese dessert features a light and fluffy sponge cake infused with the vibrant flavors of matcha green tea. It's often layered with sweetened whipped cream or red bean paste, offering a balance of bitterness and sweetness.

Matcha green tea cake is a delicious and visually stunning dessert that showcases the vibrant flavors of Japanese matcha.

This recipe combines the earthy and slightly bitter taste of matcha with the sweetness of cake for a delightful treat. Here's how you can make a matcha green tea cake:

- Recipe: Matcha Green Tea Cake
  ### - Ingredients:
    - 2 cups all-purpose flour
    - 2 tablespoons matcha green tea powder
    - 1 ½ teaspoons baking powder
    - ½ teaspoon baking soda
    - ½ teaspoon salt
    - ½ cup unsalted butter, softened
    - 1 ¼ cups granulated sugar
    - 2 large eggs
    - 1 teaspoon vanilla extract

- 1 cup buttermilk
- Whipped cream and fresh berries for garnish (optional)

- Instructions:
1. Preheat your oven to 350°F (175°C) and grease a round cake pan.

2. In a medium bowl, whisk together the flour, matcha powder, baking powder, baking soda, and salt. Set aside.

3. In a separate large bowl, cream together the softened butter and granulated sugar until light and fluffy.

4. Beat in the eggs, one at a time, followed by the vanilla extract.

5. Gradually add the dry ingredient mixture to the butter mixture, alternating with buttermilk.

Begin and end with the dry ingredients, mixing just until combined after each addition.

6. Pour the batter into the greased cake pan and smooth the top with a spatula.

7. Bake in the preheated oven for about 30-35 minutes, or until a toothpick inserted into the center comes out clean.

8. Remove the cake from the oven and let it cool in the pan for 10 minutes. Then, transfer it to a wire rack to cool completely.

9. Once the cake has cooled, you can frost it with your favorite frosting or simply dust it with powdered sugar for a lighter touch.

10. Optional: Garnish the cake with a dollop of whipped cream and fresh berries for added freshness and flavor.

11. Slice and serve the matcha green tea cake, and enjoy its unique and delightful taste.

The matcha green tea cake offers a distinct and refreshing flavor profile that is perfect for tea lovers and dessert enthusiasts alike.

Its vibrant green color and soft, moist texture make it an eye-catching centerpiece for any occasion.

Indulge in the subtle bitterness and sweet notes of this matcha-infused cake for a truly satisfying dessert experience.

iv. - Recipe: Churros with Chocolate Sauce
 - Origin: Spain
 - Description: These fried dough pastries are crispy on the outside, soft and doughy on the inside. Served with a rich and velvety chocolate sauce for dipping, they make for an irresistible sweet treat.

Churros are a beloved Mexican treat known for their crispy exterior and soft, doughy interior.

Paired with a rich and velvety chocolate sauce, they make for a delightful indulgence.

Here's a simple recipe for making churros with chocolate sauce:

- **Recipe: Churros with Chocolate Sauce**
  - **Ingredients:**
    - 1 cup water
    - 1/2 cup unsalted butter
    - 1 tablespoon granulated sugar
    - 1/4 teaspoon salt
    - 1 cup all-purpose flour
    - 3 large eggs
    - Vegetable oil, for frying

- 1/2 cup granulated sugar (for coating)
- 1 teaspoon ground cinnamon (for coating)
- 1 cup dark chocolate, chopped
- 1/2 cup heavy cream
- 1/2 teaspoon vanilla extract

- **Instructions:**
1. In a medium saucepan, combine the water, butter, sugar, and salt.

Bring the mixture to a boil over medium heat, stirring occasionally.

2. Remove the saucepan from the heat and add the flour. Stir vigorously until the mixture forms a smooth dough.

3. Beat the eggs in a separate bowl and gradually add them to the dough, mixing well after each addition, until the dough is smooth and sticky.

4. Heat vegetable oil in a large, deep saucepan or Dutch oven over medium-high heat.

The oil should be about 1 ½ to 2 inches deep.

5. Spoon the churro dough into a piping bag fitted with a large star tip.

6. Carefully pipe 4 to 6-inch long strips of dough into the hot oil, using scissors or a knife to cut the dough from the piping bag.

7. Fry the churros until golden brown and crispy, turning them occasionally to ensure even cooking.

This usually takes about 2-3 minutes per batch.

8. Remove the churros from the oil using a slotted spoon or tongs, and transfer them to a paper towel-lined plate to drain excess oil.

9. In a shallow bowl, combine the granulated sugar and ground cinnamon.

Roll the warm churros in the cinnamon-sugar mixture to coat them evenly.

10. For the chocolate sauce, place the chopped dark chocolate in a heatproof bowl.

In a small saucepan, heat the heavy cream until it simmers.

Pour the hot cream over the chocolate and let it sit for a minute. Add the vanilla extract and whisk until smooth and glossy.

11. Serve the churros warm with the chocolate sauce for dipping or drizzling.

Enjoy the crispy, cinnamon-sugar coated churros with the luscious chocolate sauce for a delightful treat.

These churros are best enjoyed fresh and warm, making them perfect for sharing with friends and family or indulging in a sweet moment of self-care.

v. - Recipe: Gulab Jamun
  - Origin: India
  - Description: These golden brown dumplings are made from milk solids and soaked in a fragrant syrup infused with cardamom, saffron, and rosewater.

With their delicate sweetness and melt-in-your-mouth texture, they are a beloved dessert in Indian cuisine.

Gulab Jamun is a popular Indian dessert known for its soft and spongy texture, soaked in a sweet syrup infused with aromatic cardamom and rose flavors.

Here's a delicious recipe to make Gulab Jamun at home:

- **Recipe: Gulab Jamun**
  - **Ingredients:**
    - 1 cup milk powder
    - 1/4 cup all-purpose flour
    - 1/4 teaspoon baking soda
    - 2 tablespoons ghee (clarified butter)
    - 3-4 tablespoons milk
    - Vegetable oil, for frying
    - 1 cup sugar
    - 1 cup water
    - 1/2 teaspoon cardamom powder
    - A few drops of rose water
    - Chopped pistachios or almonds for garnish (optional)

  - **Instructions:**
    1. In a mixing bowl, combine the milk powder, all-purpose flour, and baking soda.

Mix well to ensure there are no lumps.

    2. Add the ghee and mix until the mixture resembles coarse crumbs.

    3. Gradually add the milk, a tablespoon at a time, and knead the mixture into a soft and smooth dough.

The dough should be slightly sticky but manageable.

    4. Divide the dough into small portions and roll them into smooth balls, ensuring there are no cracks.

5. Heat vegetable oil in a deep pan or kadai over medium heat for frying.

The oil should be moderately hot, not smoking.

6. Gently slide the prepared dough balls into the hot oil, frying them in batches to avoid overcrowding.

Fry until they turn golden brown, stirring occasionally for even cooking.

This usually takes about 5-6 minutes.

7. Once the Gulab Jamun balls are fried, remove them using a slotted spoon and drain excess oil on a paper towel.

8. In a separate saucepan, combine the sugar, water, cardamom powder, and rose water.

Bring the mixture to a boil, stirring occasionally until the sugar is fully dissolved.

Simmer for an additional 5 minutes to allow the syrup to thicken slightly.

9. Remove the syrup from the heat and let it cool for a few minutes.

10. Gently drop the fried Gulab Jamun balls into the warm syrup, ensuring they are fully submerged.

Let them soak for at least 30 minutes to absorb the flavors and become soft and spongy.

11. Garnish the Gulab Jamun with chopped pistachios or almonds, if desired.

12. Serve the Gulab Jamun warm or at room temperature, allowing the syrup to soak into the balls.

Enjoy the delectable and aromatic Gulab Jamun as a sweet ending to your meal or as a special treat on festive occasions.

These soft and syrup-soaked dumplings are sure to delight your taste buds and leave you craving for more.

Conclusion:
In the world of desserts, there are no boundaries when it comes to creativity and flavor.

The sweet endings from different cultures offer a glimpse into the rich and diverse culinary traditions of the world.

 From the elegant and sophisticated to the comforting and indulgent, these desserts are sure to delight and leave a lasting impression.

So, grab your fork and embark on a sweet journey through the delectable treats of this Chapter .

Chapter 11: Conclusion

In "Flavors of the World: A Culinary Journey, through countries" we have embarked on a delightful exploration of global gastronomy, discovering the diverse flavors, techniques, and cultural traditions behind some of the world's most beloved dishes.

Throughout our culinary journey, we have experienced the rich tapestry of international cuisines, from the aromatic spices of Indian curries to the delicate flavors of Japanese sushi, the fiery heat of Mexican chilies to the fragrant herbs of Mediterranean dishes.

Embrace the Global Gastronomy:

Through this culinary adventure, we have learned that food has the power to bring people together, transcending cultural boundaries and creating connections.

Embracing the global gastronomy allows us to celebrate the diversity of flavors and experiences that the world has to offer.

It opens our palates to new tastes and textures, broadens our culinary horizons, and deepens our understanding of different cultures.

Tips for Hosting International Dinners:
To enhance your culinary journey and share the delights of global cuisine with friends and loved ones, here are some tips for hosting international dinners:

1. Research and Plan:
Choose a specific theme or country for each dinner and conduct thorough research to understand the traditional dishes, ingredients, and cooking techniques associated with that cuisine.

2. Menu Selection:
Create a well-balanced menu that includes appetizers, main courses, side dishes, and desserts representative of the chosen cuisine.

Consider dietary restrictions and preferences of your guests.

3. Authentic Ingredients:
Seek out authentic ingredients to capture the true essence of the cuisine.

Visit local international markets or specialty stores to find unique spices, sauces, and produce.

4. Recipes and Techniques:
Follow authentic recipes and learn about the traditional cooking techniques to ensure the dishes are prepared correctly.

Pay attention to details such as seasoning, spices, and presentation.

5. Table Setting and Ambiance:
Set the mood by creating a welcoming atmosphere that reflects the chosen cuisine.

Decorate the table with elements inspired by the culture, such as themed tablecloths, centerpieces, and music.

6. Sharing the Experience:
Encourage guests to share their thoughts and experiences with the food.

Engage in discussions about the flavors, origins, and cultural significance of the dishes.

7. Cultural Etiquette:

Familiarize yourself with the cultural etiquette and customs associated with the cuisine you are serving.

Respect and appreciate the traditions and dining customs of each culture.

8. Food Pairings:
Consider pairing the dishes with appropriate beverages, such as wines, spirits, or non-alcoholic options that complement the flavors and enhance the dining experience.

9. Culinary Exchange:
Encourage guests to bring a dish or ingredient representative of their own culture to create a culinary exchange and further enrich the experience.

By embracing the global gastronomy and following these tips for hosting international dinners, you can create memorable experiences, foster cultural understanding, and expand your culinary repertoire.

In conclusion, "Flavors of the World: A Culinary Journey through countries" has taken us on an exciting adventure through the diverse and delectable cuisines of different countries and regions.

From the spicy curries of India to the comforting stews of Africa, the delicate sushi of Japan to the vibrant ceviche of Peru, each dish tells a unique story and invites us to savor the flavors of the world.

So, grab your apron, gather your loved ones, and embark on your own culinary journey to explore the global flavors that await you.

Bon appétit!

Chapter 12: Appendix

In "Flavors of the World: A Culinary Journey through countries," we understand the importance of having useful resources at your fingertips to navigate the world of cooking and culinary exploration.

This appendix provides two valuable references: Conversion Charts and a Glossary of Culinary Terms, which will assist you in your culinary adventures.

Section 1: Conversion Charts:

Cooking involves precise measurements, and sometimes it's necessary to convert between different units of measurement.

The Conversion Charts provided in this appendix offer quick and easy conversions for common cooking measurements, such as volume (cups, tablespoons, teaspoons), weight (ounces, grams), and temperature (Fahrenheit and Celsius).

These charts will help ensure accuracy and consistency in your cooking endeavors.

Conversion Charts for Common Cooking Measurements

Here are the Conversion Charts for common cooking measurements:

Volume:
1 cup = 16 tablespoons = 48 teaspoons
1 tablespoon = 3 teaspoons
1 fluid ounce = 2 tablespoons = 6 teaspoons

Weight:
1 ounce = 28 grams
1 pound = 16 ounces = 454 grams

Temperature:
Fahrenheit to Celsius:
°F = (°C x 9/5) + 32

Celsius to Fahrenheit:
°C = (°F - 32) x 5/9

Please note that these conversion charts provide approximate values and should be used as a guide. It's always best to refer to specific conversion tables or use a kitchen scale for precise measurements.

Comprehensive and Detaied Conversation Chart

Here's a comprehensive and detailed conversion chart for common cooking measurements:

Volume:
1 teaspoon (tsp) = 5 milliliters (ml)
1 tablespoon (tbsp) = 15 milliliters (ml)
1 fluid ounce (fl oz) = 30 milliliters (ml)
1 cup = 240 milliliters (ml)
1 pint (pt) = 480 milliliters (ml) = 2 cups
1 quart (qt) = 960 milliliters (ml) = 4 cups
1 gallon (gal) = 3.8 liters (L) = 16 cups

Weight (Mass):
1 ounce (oz) = 28 grams (g)
1 pound (lb) = 16 ounces (oz) = 454 grams (g)
1 kilogram (kg) = 2.2 pounds (lb)

Temperature:
Fahrenheit (°F) to Celsius (°C):
$°C = (°F - 32) / 1.8$

Celsius (°C) to Fahrenheit (°F):
$°F = (°C * 1.8) + 32$

Please note that these conversion values are approximate and may vary slightly.

It's always best to refer to specific conversion tables or use a kitchen scale for precise measurements.

Extensive Conversation Chart

For a more extensive conversion chart, including measurements for common ingredients like butter, sugar, and flour, please, see below:

Here's a more extensive conversion chart for common ingredients:

Butter:
1 cup butter = 227 grams = 8 ounces = 2 sticks

Sugar:
1 cup granulated sugar = 200 grams = 7 ounces
1 cup powdered sugar = 120 grams = 4.2 ounces

Flour:
1 cup all-purpose flour = 120 grams = 4.2 ounces
1 cup cake flour = 110 grams = 3.9 ounces
1 cup whole wheat flour = 130 grams = 4.6 ounces

Brown Sugar:
1 cup packed brown sugar = 220 grams = 7.8 ounces

Liquids:
1 cup water = 240 milliliters = 8 fluid ounces
1 cup milk = 240 milliliters = 8 fluid ounces
1 cup buttermilk = 240 milliliters = 8 fluid ounces

These conversions should help you accurately measure ingredients for your recipes.

Remember that these values are approximate and may vary slightly.

It's always best to refer to specific conversion tables or use a kitchen scale for precise measurements.

Section 2: Glossary of Culinary Terms:

The culinary world has its own language, filled with specialized terms and terminology.

The Glossary of Culinary Terms in this appendix serves as a handy reference, providing definitions and explanations for a wide range of culinary terms.

Whether you encounter unfamiliar ingredients, cooking techniques, or culinary terms specific to a particular cuisine, this glossary will help you expand your culinary vocabulary and enhance your understanding of the culinary arts.

Here's a comprehensive and extensive glossary of culinary terms:

1. Julienne: To cut vegetables or other ingredients into thin, matchstick-like strips.

2. Blanch: To briefly cook ingredients in boiling water and then shock them in ice water to stop the cooking process.

3. Saute: To cook quickly over high heat in a small amount of oil or butter.

4. Deglaze: To add liquid (such as wine or broth) to a pan to loosen and dissolve the flavorful bits stuck to the bottom.

5. Caramelize: To heat sugar until it melts and turns golden brown, creating a rich, sweet flavor.

6. Braise: To cook food slowly in a covered pot with a small amount of liquid.

7. Simmer - A cooking technique that involves gently cooking food in liquid at a temperature just below boiling.

It allows flavors to meld and develop slowly.

8. Marinate: To soak food in a flavorful liquid (marinade) to enhance its flavor and tenderness.

9. Mise en place: French term meaning "everything in its place," referring to the preparation and organization of ingredients before cooking.

10. Zest: The outermost, fragrant layer of citrus peel, typically grated and used for flavoring.

11. Emulsify: To combine two or more ingredients that don't naturally mix, such as oil and vinegar, into a smooth and stable mixture.

12. Fold: To gently combine ingredients by using a spatula to lift and turn the mixture, preserving its lightness.

13. Sear: To brown the surface of food quickly at high heat, sealing in juices and adding flavor.

14. Whip: To beat ingredients vigorously with a whisk or mixer to incorporate air and create a light, fluffy texture.

15. A la carte: A menu style where each dish is listed separately with its own individual price.

16. Au gratin: A dish that is topped with breadcrumbs, cheese, or a combination of both, and then browned in the oven.

17. Baste: To spoon or brush liquid, such as marinade or pan juices, over food while it is cooking to keep it moist and add flavor.

18. Bouillon: A flavorful liquid made by simmering meat, vegetables, and aromatics, often used as a base for soups and sauces.

19. Ceviche: A dish made with raw fish or seafood marinated in citrus juice, which "cooks" the proteins without heat.

20. Chiffonade: To thinly slice or shred leafy vegetables, such as lettuce or basil, into long, thin strips.

21. Degustation: A tasting menu that features a series of small, well-presented dishes, allowing diners to sample a variety of flavors.

22. Hors d'oeuvre: Small, bite-sized appetizers served before a meal.

23. Macerate: To soak fruits or other ingredients in liquid, such as alcohol or syrup, to enhance their flavor or soften their texture.

24. Parboil: To partially cook food by boiling it briefly before finishing it in another cooking method, such as baking or frying.

25. Poach: To cook food gently in liquid, such as water or broth, just below the boiling point.

26. Reduction: To simmer a liquid, such as a sauce or broth, until it thickens and intensifies in flavor.

27. Sauté: To cook food quickly in a small amount of oil or fat over high heat, stirring or tossing frequently.

28. Sous vide: A cooking method that involves vacuum-sealing food in a plastic pouch and cooking it in a water bath at a precise temperature.

29. Culinary: The term "culinary" refers to anything related to cooking, food preparation, and the art of preparing and presenting food.

It encompasses a wide range of activities, techniques, and skills involved in creating and serving meals.

The culinary field includes various aspects such as cooking methods, recipe development, ingredient selection, flavor combinations, culinary traditions, and culinary arts.

It involves not only the practical skills of cooking but also the knowledge and understanding of different cuisines, culinary techniques, and food culture.

Overall, "culinary" relates to the culinary arts and the pursuit of creating delicious and aesthetically pleasing meals.

This comprehensive and extensive glossary provides definitions for a wide range of culinary terms commonly used in cooking and baking.

It can serve as a valuable reference for home cooks and aspiring chefs, helping them navigate the world of food and enhance their culinary skills.

This glossary provides definitions for key culinary terms commonly used in cooking and baking.

It can be a handy reference for understanding and executing various cooking techniques.

Glossary of Other Terms:

1. Gastronomy - The art and science of good eating, encompassing the study of food, culture, and culinary techniques.

2. Fusion Cuisine - A culinary style that combines elements of different culinary traditions or cuisines to create innovative and unique dishes.

3. Ingredients - The components used in a recipe to create a dish.

They can include food items such as vegetables, meat, spices, and herbs.

4. Flavor - The sensory perception of taste and aroma in food.

It encompasses the combination of various taste sensations, including sweet, sour, salty, bitter, and umami.

5. Cuisine - A characteristic style of cooking and food preparation associated with a particular region or culture.

6. Palate - The roof of the mouth, which plays a vital role in taste perception. It also refers to an individual's ability to taste and appreciate flavors.

7. Texture - The physical consistency or feel of food in the mouth, such as smooth, crunchy, creamy, or chewy.

8. Presentation - The visual arrangement and display of food on a plate or platter.

It involves the use of techniques, colors, and garnishes to enhance the aesthetic appeal of a dish.

9. Garnish - Decorative elements added to a dish before serving to enhance its visual appeal.

Garnishes can include herbs, sauces, edible flowers, or other complementary ingredients.

10. Sauté - A cooking technique that involves quickly frying or browning food in a small amount of oil or fat over high heat.

11. Deglaze - The process of adding liquid, such as wine or broth, to a pan to dissolve and scrape up the browned bits of food stuck to the bottom.

It is done to create a flavorful sauce or base.

12. Emulsify - To combine two or more immiscible liquids, such as oil and vinegar, using an emulsifying agent to create a stable mixture.

13. Infuse - To steep or soak a liquid, such as water or oil, with flavors from herbs, spices, or other aromatic ingredients.

14. Braise - A cooking technique that involves searing food in hot oil and then slow-cooking it in a covered pot with a small amount of liquid, resulting in tender and flavorful dishes.

15. Sous Vide - A cooking method that involves vacuum-sealing food in a plastic bag and cooking it at a precise temperature in a water bath, ensuring even and consistent cooking.

16. Artisan - Referring to food or products that are handmade or produced in small batches by skilled craftsmen, often using traditional methods.

17. Locally Sourced - Referring to food ingredients that are sourced or produced within a specific geographic region, typically to support local farmers and reduce carbon footprint.

18. Sustainability - The practice of using resources in a way that preserves ecological balance and minimizes environmental impact, often applied to food production and sourcing.

19. Buen provecho
The phrase "Buen provecho" is a Spanish expression that translates to "Enjoy your meal" or "Bon appétit" in English. It is commonly used in Spanish-speaking countries to wish someone a good and enjoyable meal before they start eating. The correct spelling of the phrase is "Buen provecho" with a capital "B" at the beginning.

Please note that this glossary includes terms that are not strictly culinary but may be relevant and useful in the context of understanding the broader aspects of food, cooking, and culinary culture.

By having access to Conversion Charts and a Glossary of Culinary Terms, you'll have valuable resources at your disposal to confidently navigate through various recipes, experiment with new ingredients, and better understand the culinary techniques employed in different cuisines.

With these resources at hand, you can embark on your culinary journey with confidence, embracing the world of flavors and expanding your culinary skills.

Remember, cooking is an art form that knows no boundaries, and with the knowledge and tools provided in this appendix, you can embark on your own culinary adventures with ease.

Happy cooking, exploring, and savoring the diverse and delectable flavors of the world!

Chapter 13: Recipe Index

Here is the recipe index for "Flavors of the World: A Culinary Journey" book.

It provides a convenient reference to all the recipes featured in the book, organized by chapter and section.

- Red Curry
- Massaman Curry
- Panang Curry

- Section 2: Thai Noodles
  - Pad Thai
  - Pad See Ew
  - Drunken Noodles (Pad Kee Mao)
  - Tom Yum Noodle Soup

Chapter 4: Indian Spices and Curries
- Section 1: Indian Curries
  - Butter Chicken
  - Lamb Rogan Josh
  - Chana Masala (Chickpea Curry)
  - Palak Paneer (Spinach and Cottage Cheese Curry)

- Section 2: Indian Spices
  - Garam Masala
  - Curry Powder
  - Tandoori Masala
  - Rasam Powder

Chapter 5: African Flavors
- Section 1: Moroccan Tagines and Couscous
  - Moroccan Tagine
  - Moroccan Couscous

- Section 2: Ethiopian Injera and Doro Wat
  - Injera
  - Doro Wat

- Section 3: South African Braai and Bobotie
  - Braai
  - Bobotie

- Section 4: Nigerian Jollof Rice and Suya

- Jollof Rice
- Suya

Chapter 6: Latin American Delights
- Section 1: Mexican Tacos and Guacamole
  - Tacos
  - Guacamole

- Section 2: Argentinian Asado and Empanadas
  - Asado
  - Empanadas

- Section 3: Brazilian Feijoada and Brigadeiros
  - Feijoada
  - Brigadeiros

- Section 4: Peruvian Ceviche and Lomo Saltado
  - Ceviche
  - Lomo Saltado

Chapter 7: Middle Eastern Cuisine
- Section 1: Lebanese Mezze and Shawarma
  - Baba Ganoush
  - Tabbouleh
  - Falafel
  - Shawarma

- Section 2: Turkish Kebabs and Baklava
  - Kebabs
  - Baklava

- Section 3: Israeli Falafel and Hummus
  - Falafel
  - Hummus

- Section 4: Iranian Kabobs and Tahdig
  - Kabobs

- Tahdig

Chapter 8: Oceanic Tastes

- Section 1: Australian BBQ and Pavlova
  - Australian BBQ
  - Pavlova

- Section 2: New Zealand Hangi and Kiwi Pies
  - New Zealand Hangi
  - Kiwi Pies

- Section 3: Hawaiian Poke and Huli Huli Chicken
  - Hawaiian Poke
  - Huli Huli Chicken

- Section 4: Polynesian Luau and Samoan Palusami
  - Polynesian Luau
  - Samoan Palusami

Chapter 9: Fusion Fare
- Section 1: Blending Flavors from Around the World
  - Fusion Recipe 1
  - Fusion Recipe 2
  - Fusion Recipe 3

- Section 2: Creative Recipes and Innovations
  - Creative Recipe 1
  - Creative Recipe 2
  - Creative Recipe 3

Chapter 10: Sweet Endings
- Section 1: Decadent Desserts from Different Cultures
  - French Patisserie
  - Italian Gelato
  - Japanese Wagashi

- Indian Mithai
- Turkish Delights
- Arabic Baklava
- Mexican Churros
- Brazilian Brigadeiros
- Tiramisu
- Baklava
- Matcha Green Tea Cake
- Churros with Chocolate Sauce
- Gulab Jamun

Chapter 11: Conclusion
- Embrace the Global Gastronomy
- Tips for Hosting International Dinners

Chapter 12: Appendix
- Conversion Charts
- Glossary of Culinary Terms

Chapter 13: Recipe Index

Please note that this is a sample index and may not include all the recipes mentioned in the book.

Comprehensive List of Recipes by Country:

1. Japanese Cuisine:
   - Sushi Delights
     - Classic Sushi Rolls
     - Nigiri Sushi
     - Tempura Rolls
     - Miso Soup
     - Ramen Noodle Bowls
       - Tonkotsu Ramen

- Shoyu Ramen
- Miso Ramen
- Spicy Tan Tan Ramen

2. Thai Cuisine:
   - Fragrant Thai Curries and Noodles
     - Green Curry
     - Red Curry
     - Massaman Curry
     - Panang Curry
     - Pad Thai
     - Pad See Ew
     - Drunken Noodles (Pad Kee Mao)
     - Tom Yum Noodle Soup

3. Indian Cuisine:
   - Indian Spices and Curries
     - Butter Chicken
     - Lamb Rogan Josh
     - Chana Masala (Chickpea Curry)
     - Palak Paneer (Spinach and Cottage Cheese Curry)
     - Garam Masala
     - Curry Powder
     - Tandoori Masala
     - Rasam Powder

4. Latin American Cuisine:
   - Latin American Delights
     - Mexican Tacos and Guacamole
     - Argentinian Asado and Empanadas
     - Brazilian Feijoada and Brigadeiros
     - Peruvian Ceviche and Lomo Saltado
     - Churros with Chocolate Sauce

5. Middle Eastern Cuisine:
   - Lebanese Mezze and Shawarma
     - Baba Ganoush

- Tabbouleh
- Falafel
- Shawarma
- Turkish Kebabs and Baklava
- Israeli Falafel and Hummus
- Iranian Kabobs and Tahdig

6. African Cuisine:
   - Moroccan Tagines and Couscous
   - Ethiopian Injera and Doro Wat
   - South African Braai and Bobotie
   - Nigerian Jollof Rice and Suya

7. Oceanic Cuisine:
   - Australian BBQ and Pavlova
   - New Zealand Hangi and Kiwi Pies
   - Hawaiian Poke and Huli Huli Chicken
   - Polynesian Luau and Samoan Palusami

8. Fusion Fare:
   - Blending Flavors from Around the World
   - Creative Recipes and Innovations

9. Sweet Endings:
   - Decadent Desserts from Different Cultures
     - French Patisserie
       - Croissants
       - Macarons
     - Italian Gelato
       - Vanilla Gelato
       - Pistachio Gelato
     - Japanese Wagashi
       - Dorayaki
       - Matcha Mochi
     - Indian Mithai
       - Gulab Jamun
       - Jalebi

- Turkish Delights
  - Baklava
  - Turkish Delight
- Arabic Baklava
  - Pistachio Baklava
  - Walnut Baklava
- Mexican Churros
  - Classic Cinnamon Sugar Churros
  - Filled Churros with Chocolate Sauce
- Brazilian Brigadeiros
  - Chocolate Brigadeiros
  - Coconut Brigadeiros
- Tiramisu
- Matcha Green Tea Cake
- Churros with Chocolate Sauce
- Gulab Jamun

This list provides an overview of all the recipes in the book categorized by their respective countries or cuisines.

Author's Note

Dear Readers,

It is with great pleasure that I present to you "Flavors of the World: A Culinary Journey through countries"

This book has been a labor of love, inspired by my passion for exploring diverse cuisines and experiencing the rich tapestry of flavors that our world has to offer.

Through this culinary journey, I hope to transport you to different corners of the globe and ignite your taste buds with a myriad of exotic and tantalizing dishes.

In "Flavors of the World," I have carefully curated a collection of recipes that represent the essence of each culture, highlighting their unique ingredients, cooking techniques, and traditional dishes.

From the vibrant spices of India to the delicate artistry of Japanese cuisine, each chapter invites you to delve into the culinary heritage of various countries.

Through this book, I encourage you to embrace the beauty of cultural diversity and the unifying power of food.

As you embark on this culinary adventure, I invite you to step out of your comfort zone and explore new flavors, experiment with unfamiliar ingredients, and embrace the joy of cooking with an open mind and a curious palate.

To enhance your cooking experience, I have included helpful conversion charts and a glossary of culinary terms in the appendix.

These resources will assist you in navigating the world of international recipes and understanding the terminology commonly used in the kitchen.

I would like to express my gratitude to the countless chefs, home cooks, and culinary enthusiasts who have shared their knowledge and passion for their respective cuisines.

Your dedication to preserving culinary traditions and pushing the boundaries of creativity has been an inspiration throughout the writing process.

I hope that "Flavors of the World: A Culinary Journey through countries" will not only be a source of delightful recipes but also a gateway to cultural exploration and appreciation.

May it inspire you to embark on your own culinary adventures, creating memories and connections through the universal language of food.

Happy cooking and bon appétit!

Sincerely,

Okongor Ndifon

Made in the USA
Las Vegas, NV
03 December 2024

18aaeed6-f629-42aa-939c-714215d642c5R01